Alain Robbe-Grillet

Twayne's World Authors Series

Maxwell A. Smith, Editor
Guerry Professor of French, Emeritus
The University of Chattanooga
Former Visiting Professor in Modern Languages
The Florida State University

TWAS 682

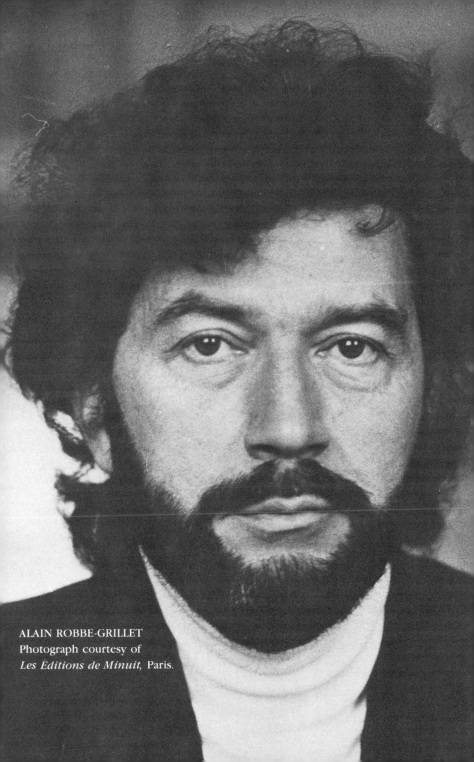

ALAIN ROBBE-GRILLET
Photograph courtesy of
Les Éditions de Minuit, Paris.

Alain Robbe-Grillet

By Ilona Leki

The University of Tennessee

Twayne Publishers • *Boston*

Alain Robbe-Grillet

Ilona Leki

Copyright © 1983 by G. K. Hall & Company
All Rights Reserved
Published by Twayne Publishers
A Division of G. K. Hall & Company
70 Lincoln Street
Boston, Massachusetts 02111

Book Production by Marne B. Sultz
Book Design by Barbara Anderson

Printed on permanent/durable acid-free
paper and bound in The United States
of America.

Library of Congress Cataloging in Publication Data

Leki, Ilona.
  Alain Robbe-Grillet.

  (Twayne's world authors series ;
TWAS 682)
  Bibliography: p. 179
  Includes index.
  1. Robbe-Grillet, Alain, 1922–
—Criticism and interpretation.
I. Title. II. Series.
PQ2635.0117Z72   843.'914   82-15654
ISBN 0-8057-6529-8

Contents

About the Author

Ilona Leki received the Ph.D. from the University of Illinois. She has taught at the Lycée de Saint-Cloud in Paris, the University of Illinois, and Knoxville College and teaches at present in the Department of English at the University of Tennessee. She has held a French Government Grant and has been a participant in the National Endowment for the Humanities Summer Seminar program. Professor Leki works as a French language translator for the United States government and has also published articles and presented papers on Henri Michaux, Jean Genet, and Alain Robbe-Grillet as well as on foreign language teaching methodology.

Preface

At a discussion which took place after a showing of Alain Robbe-Grillet's film *L'Eden et après*, a student vehemently accused Robbe-Grillet of antifeminism, pointing out the film's many gratuitous scenes of female nudity in a violent context. Robbe-Grillet, who had just been outlining his progressive positions on politics and social relations, jumped to his feet shouting that one of the few English words he recognized was the word "woman" and that when this word was spoken with vehemence by someone who had just seen one of his films, he always knew what he was being accused of. If he had a defense already prepared, it is because his work has so often been attacked on a wide variety of grounds over the thirty years of his literary life. The vigor of his struggle to combat his opponents' objections has given him the reputation of being a literary and intellectual terrorist. Despite the fact that his boisterous combativeness has tempered somewhat over the years, his dark curly hair and beard and his mocking attitude still suggest the iconoclast. Nevertheless the impact on contemporary French literature that Robbe-Grillet and his colleagues, "an association of malefactors," as Natalie Sarraute called them tongue-in-cheek, is undeniable. The emergence of the French New Novel in the 1950s, with Robbe-Grillet as the form's leading theoretician, altered the climate in French literary circles such that any serious writer after Robbe-Grillet must in some way come to terms with his innovations and challenges to the traditional novel form.

Different novels lend themselves more readily to one critical approach than to others. I have tried to keep this in mind in this study of Alain Robbe-Grillet, and my approach to the novels has been eclectic. I have offered suggestions for various readings of his works, trying never to suggest that only one reading was possible or desirable. My goal has been clarity so that students of literature not familiar with Robbe-Grillet will not become frustrated in attempting to deal with his disconcerting novels. This study is meant to be a guide. I have at the same time, however, avoided an analysis of Robbe-Grillet's work which might recuperate it, that is, which might strip his nontraditional texts of their radicality and of their challenges to traditional fictional patterns by attempting to impose on the nontraditional text traditional fiction's concern with causality, chronology, psychology, philosophy, etc. I have made no attempt to reassure the reader by insisting that Robbe-Grillet's texts do correspond to acceptable and familiar patterns of development, but instead have worked toward a range of interpretations in accord with the whole thrust of Robbe-Grillet's contradictory, disconcerting art.

Since not all readers will be familiar with all of Robbe-Grillet's texts, the summaries of the novels discussed are sometimes rather long in order to permit the reader to follow more readily the subsequent analyses of the works. In addition, portions of those summaries are disjointed and contradict other portions. I have made no attempt to eliminate these narrative jolts, preferring instead to be faithful to the original texts. On the other hand, eliminations must be made in any study of limited length, and therefore, in certain cases when material of secondary importance is not discussed in the analysis, it will not be mentioned in the summary either.

Despite Robbe-Grillet's importance as a cinematographer and the importance he himself attaches to his work in film, it was not possible to include extensive analyses of the individual films, and I have therefore preferred to limit my remarks to a general discussion of the place of cinema in Robbe-Grillet's creative work. The limited length of this discussion should not be seen as proportionate to the importance of the subject.

Furthermore, I have not included in the text of this study or in the bibliography many of the short texts or uncollected articles Robbe-Grillet has published. Complete references to these can be found in the more extensive bibliographies mentioned in the selected bibliography published here. On the other hand, I have tried to include in the bibliography books and articles which would give the reader a rather wide range of approaches to Robbe-Grillet, from essentialist and humanist to phenomenological and generative approaches. In order to give the reader some idea of Robbe-Grillet as a personality I have included references to a few particularly helpful interviews. Finally, I have had to omit references to many excellent articles on Robbe-Grillet, particularly by American academicians; the reader is again referred to the more extensive bibliographies on this author.

Reference to the *Archives du 20ème siècle* in the bibliography indicates the series *Archives du 20ème siècle* created for French television by Jean José Marchand (Copyright SFP, 1971). I would like to thank Monsieur Marchand for the use of this material. I would also like to express my gratitude to Alain Robbe-Grillet for his friendliness and interest in my work, to Michel Rybalka and the National Endowment for the Humanities for giving me the time and support necessary to complete this project, and most especially to my best friend, Paul Barrette, for his moral support and his inexhaustible faith in me.

Ilona Leki

The University of Tennessee

Chronology

1922   18 August: Alain Robbe-Grillet born to Yvonne Canu and Gaston Robbe-Grillet in Saint-Pierre-Quilbinion near Brest in Brittany.

1922–1939   Attended the local school, then the Lycée Buffon in Paris.

1939   First baccalaureate in mathematics and natural science from the Lycée Saint-Louis in Paris.

1941   Second baccalaureate degree in math from the Lycée de Brest.

1941–1942   Attended the Institut National Agronomique ("French National Institute of Agronomy") in Paris under the German occupation.

1942   Taken with his entire class at the Institut Agronomique to work on lathes and milling machines in a German factory in Nuremberg.

1943   Fell ill with an infectious rheumatism and sent back to a hospital in Paris.

1946   Graduated from the Institut Agronomique. Went to work for the Institut National de la Statistique et des Etudes économiques ("National Institute of Statistics").

1948   Quit his job with the Institut National de la Statistique and went to work for his sister in her laboratory in Seine et Marne at the Chateau de Bois Boudran.

1949   Completed *Un Régicide*. Found a job in biology and statistics with the Institut des Fruits et Agrumes Coloniaux ("Institute of Colonial Fruits and Crops") as an overseer of banana plantations.

1949–1951 Left for the French West Indies, Martinique, and Guadeloupe after a stop in Guinea (Africa).

1951–1952 Fell ill in Martinique and wrote *Les Gommes* on the boat on his way back to France. First book reviews appeared in *Critique* (November 1951). Met Jérôme Lindon at Les Editions de Minuit.

1953 *Les Gommes* appeared with Les Editions de Minuit.

1954 Prix Fénéon for *Les Gommes*. Roland Barthes's important article on *Les Gommes*, "Littérature objective," appeared in *Critique*.

1955 *Le Voyeur* appeared and received the Prix des Critiques. First article on literary theory, "A quoi servent les théories," published in *L'Express*. Took the job of literary consultant at Les Editions de Minuit, a position he still holds.

1956 Awarded a grant from the Foundation del Duca. Theoretical article, "Une Voie pour le roman futur," appeared in Jean Paulhan's *Nouvelle Nouvelle Revue Française*.

1957 Published *La Jalousie*, generally termed unreadable; 23 October: married Catherine Rstakian.

1958 "Nature, humanisme, tragédie" appeared in the *Nouvelle Nouvelle Revue Française*.

1959 Published *Dans le labyrinthe*, which was very well received. Offered the opportunity to work on the film that became *L'Immortelle*.

1960 Collaborated with Alain Resnais on *L'Année dernière à Marienbad*. Signed the *Manifeste des 121*. Became a member of the Comité supérieure des programmes de la télévision ("Television Programming Committee").

1961 *L'Année dernière à Marienbad* presented at the Venice Film Festival, where it won the Prix du Lion d'or, and in France, where it won the Méliès Prize. Robbe-Grillet's first *ciné-roman, L'Année dernière à Marienbad,* appeared.

1962   Published *Instantanés*, a collection of short fiction pieces written over a ten-year span.

1963   *L'Immortelle*, the first film he wrote and directed himself, opened in Paris; the *ciné-roman* of *L'Immortelle* appeared in the same year. *Pour un nouveau roman*, a collection of his critical articles, published by Les Editions de Minuit. Bruce Morrissette's important study of Robbe-Grillet's work, *Les Romans d'Alain Robbe-Grillet*, appeared in France.

1964   *Pour un nouveau roman* published in Gallimard's paperback series Idées. Robbe-Grillet's first trip to the United States, on a lecture tour of a number of American universities.

1965   *La Maison de rendez-vous*.

1966   *Trans-Europ-Express* opened in Paris. Named a member of the Haut Comité pour la défense et l'expansion de la langue française ("Committee for the Defense and Promotion of the French Language").

1968   *L'Homme qui ment* opened.

1969   Appearances on French television.

1970   Both *Projet pour une révolution à New York*, a novel, and *L'Eden et après*, his first color film, appeared. Retrospective festivals of Robbe-Grillet's films organized in France and England. First collaborative work outside of film published in the film periodical *Zoom*, "La Demeure immobile de David Hamilton."

1971   *N a pris les dés* completed and sold to French television network. Participated in conference on the New Novel organized at Cerisy-la-Salle. *Rêves des jeunes filles*, a collaboration with David Hamilton, appeared.

1972   *Les Demoiselles d'Hamilton* with David Hamilton appeared. Spent a term teaching at New York University. Made contact with Roy Lichtenstein, Robert Rauschenberg, and the New York avant-garde art community.

1973   Resumed painting for first time since youth.

1974   *Glissements progressifs du plaisir* appeared; in Italy Robbe-Grillet was prosecuted and the film was closed down, accused of being pornographic.

1975   *Topologie d'une cité fantôme* published, including texts from Robbe-Grillet's collaborations with Rauschenberg, Hamilton, and Paul Delvaux and texts based on paintings by René Magritte. *Le Jeu avec le feu* opened. *N a pris les dés* finally appeared on French television. Published *Construction d'un temple en ruines à la Déesse Vanadé* with etchings by Delvaux. Ten-day colloquium organized on Robbe-Grillet at Cerisy-la-Salle. Taught another term at New York University. Received into the French Legion of Honor (*Chevalier de la Légion d'Honneur*). Published *La Belle Captive,* with paintings by Magritte.

1976   Outline of the structure of a new film, *Pièges à fourrure,* appeared in *Minuit.*

1977   *Temple aux miroirs,* a collaboration with photographer Irina Ionesco, published with Seghers.

1978   Publication of *Souvenirs d'un triangle d'or* and *Un Régicide,* Robbe-Grillet's first novel. Taught at the University of California at Los Angeles. *Traces suspectes en surfaces,* a collaboration with Rauschenberg, exhibited in American museums.

1979   Taught at New York University. Continued to work on an imaginary autobiography, a part of which appeared in *Minuit,* "Fragment autobiographique imaginaire."

1981   Published *Le Rendez-vous,* a detective story based on grammatical features of French as generators of the text for an intermediate French reader for American students. Published this text in France as *Djinn, un trou rouge entre les pavés disjoints.*

Chapter One

The Beginnings of a New Novel

Perhaps the most spirited literary debates in France since the days of Surrealism centered around the appearance of what came to be called the French New Novel, the Nouveau Roman. Much of the original controversy in the 1950s over the value of this literature focused on the novels and the theoretical and critical writing in defense of the Nouveau Roman by Alain Robbe-Grillet. When his first published novel, *Les Gommes,* appeared in 1953, critics objected that Robbe-Grillet could not tell an ordinary detective story simply and naturally, that his characters were unconvincing, that his long descriptions of ordinary objects constituted an ill-advised attempt to turn literature into geometry, into science. Other defenders, theoreticians and novelists, soon took up the debate and the Nouveau Roman became an important literary phenomenon. Among the explicators was critic and writer Roland Barthes; among the defenders, the leftist intellectual avant-garde; among the practitioners of this new art, a disparate group of writers associated with the Nouveau Roman by critics in an ultimately unsuccessful attempt to limit and define a literary school. Such a school would have had to accommodate the interests, techniques, and explorations of writers as different as Natalie Sarraute, Michel Butor, and Claude Simon; their work resisted the categorization. But each of these writers, beginning as far back as Sarraute in *Tropismes* in 1938, questioned the novel form as it had been handed down to them from the nineteenth century.

In Robbe-Grillet's analysis the typical nineteenth-century novelist, the artist, had something to say; he was in possession of

1

a truth which he felt he had to and could transpose into the novel and communicate to his readers. This self-assurance was a reflection of what was considered the legitimate rise to power of the bourgeoisie, who like the aristocrats before them justified their rank by claiming it was natural and inevitable. Similarly the nineteenth-century novelist, epitomized by Honoré de Balzac, Robbe-Grillet's *bête noire,* did not question the codified system of literature. If stories were told in a particular way, it was because that was the natural way to tell a story. These views proved to be extremely tenacious, and by the 1950s in France, of all the arts, only the novel continued to be doggedly representational. The twentieth-century novel was amazingly closer to the nineteenth-century novel than twentieth-century music and painting were to nineteenth-century music and painting. In fact by the last third of the nineteenth century Cézanne thought of his painting as research and Van Gogh was embarrassed to use the word artist to refer to himself.[1] Painters had rejected the idea that art reflects a preexisting reality, the reality of the real world, a message from the gods, or an inspired intuition flowing directly from the soul of the artist, and already spoke of their art as work, as production. Nevertheless, despite challenges to the traditional novel form by a stream of writers in whose steps the New Novel follows—Flaubert, Joyce, Proust, Faulkner, Kafka, Roussel, Beckett—the general view of the novel as form and not as representation did not come in France until many decades later. No doubt some of the novel's sluggishness is attributable to distinctions between prose and poetry like that made by Sartre in *Qu'est-ce que la littérature,* where he defines poetry as opaque, as work on and with language, and prose as language which is itself transparent, allowing one form of reality to be translated into another, to transmit a message.

The literary and intellectual climate into which Robbe-Grillet entered as a novelist was dominated by the *littérature engagée* of Sartre and Malraux and the literature of the absurd of Camus. At that time Sartre's and Malraux's understanding of the function of literature differed little from that of Zola or Balzac. Literature was placed within the context of a given social or philosophical order; the writer's task was to capture the position of man within the order. At issue was man's comprehension of his own freedom and his acceptance of responsibility within a world which, but for this acceptance, can only be tragic. Camus's world on the other hand was not tragic but absurd; absurdity lay in the gap between the independent existence of things in the world and man's basic desire to have those things exist only in relation to him.

Phenomenology had had a certain impact on existentialist and absurdist literature, which did reflect a willingness to regard the world as phenomenon. Yet there were contradictions between the implications of phenomenological views of the world and the philosophical underpinnings of existential and absurdist literature. In the context of the phenomenologist's position that it is only in consciousness of phenomena that such phenomena exist, the world necessarily loses its tragedy and its absurdity. Tragedy and absurdity exist not in the world but in the intentionality of the perceiver's gaze. The world itself merely is. But neither Sartre nor Camus really wanted to bracket the old humanistic world of tragedy and absurdity. Like Balzac, they too had truths to express.

The Early Years

Any stagnation in the art of the novel was certainly not apparent to the young Robbe-Grillet. The family had moved from the Jura region in France near the Swiss border to Saint-Pierre-Quilbinion in Brittany, which at the time of Robbe-Grillet's birth was a rural region eventually incorporated into the city of Brest. Although Robbe-Grillet never lived for any extended period of time in either region, on his young mind were imprinted images of the gently rolling hills of the Jura and the rocky, foggy Breton coastline, both images which were later to emerge in his writing. Like all academically successful students at the time, Robbe-Grillet studied Greek and Latin as a schoolboy, but he eventually went into a mathematics curriculum in high school in Paris. Although as a child he had shown interest in modern music and art and had even tried his hand at painting, and although he had read Kafka, Faulkner, and Graham Greene and had been exposed

to the standard French literary classics during his elementary-
and secondary-school studies, he did not come from a literary
background. His father, his sister, and his friends were all en-
gineers or scientists. Furthermore, he had never felt particularly
drawn to literature. Instead, interested in botany, he had imagined for himself the life of a ranger, out in the open air all day
caring for plants.

After receiving two baccalaureate degrees, in mathematics and
in natural science, Robbe-Grillet enrolled at the French National
Institute of Agronomy in 1941 under the German occupation.
But in 1942 he was taken to Nuremberg to work in a German
factory. There he served an apprenticeship in machining and
eventually received a certificate of completion. Into his middle
twenties Robbe-Grillet still showed no sign of any particular
interest in literature; he had written a handful of poems during
the war, a conventional short story of young love set in Brest,
and a diary account of an unsatisfactory postwar Communist youth
expedition to Bulgaria, where he spent a few days in 1947 helping
to build a railroad. After completing his degree in agricultural
engineering, he began his publishing career with an article called
"Possibilité du cheptel bovin" [Livestock Possibilities] written
during the time he worked for the National Institute of Statistics
(1946–48). Robbe-Grillet has often said that it was his fortuitous
lack of training in literature which saved him from absorbing the
prevailing restrictive literary conventions and thus made it possible for him to conceive of new literary forms, forms recognized
as incorrect by those with more extensive knowledge of literature
than he had.

Robbe-Grillet's first sustained effort in literature took place
during the period when he worked part time as a scientist in his
sister's laboratory doing hormone experiments in biology. He had
left his regular office job at the National Institute of Statistics
to take this part-time, low-paying job because he had been taken
by the desire to write a novel. Since this job with his sister left
him a great deal of spare time, he was able to write *Un Régicide*,
his first novel, completed in 1949. He submitted his manuscript
of *Un Régicide* to the important French publisher Gallimard, left

his sister's laboratory, and through the Association des Anciens Elèves de l'Institut Agronomique looked for a regular job. He soon found work with the Institute of Colonial Fruits and Crops, which sent him to banana plantations in France's colonial holdings in the West Indies, where he worked tending banana trees. In Fort-de-France, Martinique, Robbe-Grillet lived in a house which was later to serve as the model, transformed by imagination and time, for the terraced colonial-style house in *La Jalousie*. But in 1951 he fell ill and spent some time in a hospital in Guadeloupe. Again faced with a large amount of leisure time, as he had been in his sister's laboratory, he read for the first time the New Testament (which he has called a precursor of the New Novel) and mulled over ideas for a second novel, which he completed during his boat trip back to France from the tropics.

Upon his return to Paris he inquired at Gallimard about his *Régicide* manuscript and learned that it had been sent on to another publisher more interested in nontraditional works, Les Editions de Minuit, which was seriously considering publishing it. He suggested, however, that they instead look over his second manuscript, *Les Gommes,* which they accepted for immediate publication, thus signaling in effect the end of his career as an agricultural engineer, the inauguration of his career as a writer, and his long association with Jérôme Lindon and Les Editions de Minuit.

Despite the fact that *Les Gommes* (1953) was rather poorly received by the public and the general press, the book did arouse some enthusiasm in literary magazines; there was a favorable article by French writer Jean Cayrol, for example, and the novel received the Prix Fénéon. During this time Robbe-Grillet was working irregularly for the Assemblée permanente des Présidents de Chambre d'Agriculture, making just enough money to survive. In 1955 Lindon offered Robbe-Grillet the position of literary consultant at Les Editions de Minuit; with that income, plus sympathy and some financial support from his family, he was free to pursue his literary interests.

It was his second book, *Le Voyeur,* that brought him into literary prominence, partly because of the storm it created among the judges from the Prix des Critiques, which was awarded to *Le Voyeur* in 1955. Supported by the more modern members of the jury, Georges Bataille, Jean Paulhan, and Maurice Blanchot, *Le Voyeur* was strongly denounced by prominent and more traditional critics, Emile Henriot, Roger Kemp, and Gabriel Marcel, who went so far as to resign from the committee over this dispute.[2] As far as the detractors were concerned, *Le Voyeur* was not even a novel; it lacked what all novels must have and included what all novels must eliminate. In view of the fact that the award had been made the previous year to Françoise Sagan, and that this novel was radically different from the literary tradition that produced Sagan, it is not surprising that *Le Voyeur* elicited strong negative reactions from members of the awards committee. Henriot published a long article in the respected French newspaper *Le Monde* attacking *Le Voyeur* as immoral, its main character as insane.[3] But these disputes and the publicity they received created curiosity about the book and resulted in the sale of 10,000 copies in the first year, a large number for the relatively unknown Robbe-Grillet.

By this time Robbe-Grillet had decided to devote himself entirely to a literary career and had completely given up agronomy as a profession. He had become acquainted with a number of literary critics and began writing letters to them and pursuing conversations with them at various gatherings explaining his conception of the novel, and winning over, if not by his literary theory and practice at least by the enthusiasm of his personality, such detractors as Emile Henriot, who was then instrumental in securing for Robbe-Grillet a grant from the Fondation del Duca.

Robbe-Grillet was also winning over a young actress, Catherine Rstakian, whom he had met on a train to Istanbul. In 1957 they married; since then Catherine Robbe-Grillet has worked closely with Robbe-Grillet on all his films, appearing in most of them and shooting the stills on set.

Made aware of Robbe-Grillet's writing, perhaps by Cayrol, in 1954, Roland Barthes published an important article, "Littérature objective," in the journal *Critique* on *Les Gommes* which did a great deal to help the career of the young novelist. Barthes became an enthusiastic supporter of Robbe-Grillet and his article on *Les Gommes* and another later on *Le Voyeur* had an influence both on Robbe-Grillet's theoretical work and on his subsequent novels. In "Littérature objective," Barthes pointed out that Robbe-Grillet's long intricate descriptions of surfaces were not background against which a story was told but rather the very bases out of which the story lines emerged; these story lines were already of secondary importance in the first novels and became increasingly problematic and insignificant throughout this first period of Robbe-Grillet's writing. Robbe-Grillet's writing had achieved a kind of neutrality which Barthes applauded as honest and truly literary. Barthes's important analyses of this new approach to the novel served as a rallying point for Robbe-Grillet's supporters and offered the first coherent strategies for reading his works.

But Barthes's use of the term "littérature objective" led to a certain amount of confusion despite his attempt to minimize this confusion by suggesting the neologism "littérature objectale" as a more accurate designation for this new literature. By this term he meant a literature directed toward the object rather than toward the subject as a lens (*objectif* in French) is turned toward an object. But he was misunderstood to mean instead literature that is objective in the impossible sense of uninterpretive of reality, distanced from reality, impassive and impartial. This misinterpretation lent fuel to the criticism of Robbe-Grillet's writing as overly scientific, cold, inhuman, and sterile.

Nevertheless, Robbe-Grillet was far from alone in his rebellion and experimentation during this period. Positive responses of critics he respected, like Barthes, confirmed him in his belief that there was a reading public which had become dissatisfied with the novel as it existed at the time. Other novelists also felt uncomfortable with the traditional novel, and the press quickly began to group together a number of these writers of increasingly "unreadable" texts: Natalie Sarraute (whose essays in *L'Ere du soupçon* from 1956 echoed many of Robbe-Grillet's concerns about the novel), Michel Butor, Claude Ollier (whom Robbe-Grillet had met in the 1940s in Bulgaria), Claude Simon, Robert Pinget. The fact that Les Editions de Minuit became the main publisher

for these experimental writers further served to imply a homo-
geneity among them which in fact never existed. Their literary
concerns were quite disparate, as they soon found during sessions
they organized at this time to discuss privately their respective
literary interests. The one thing they did have in common was
critical rejection of their work on the grounds that they were in
fact not writing novels because they had failed to reproduce the
techniques of the great novelists of the past: time was in disorder,
the books had no structure, the characters were not convincing.
Although the authors concerned sometimes objected to being
lumped together under the appelation, the term Nouveau Roman
became fashionable on the Parisian literary scene and the contro-
versies surrounding the Nouveau Roman were good publicity to
promote the sale of the books to a French public always eager to
debate new intellectual issues.

But even Barthes, like others who were beginning to follow
this new literature, was somewhat taken aback by Robbe-Grillet's
third novel, *La Jalousie* (1957).[4] The objectal or objective critical
approach was no longer appropriate for *La Jalousie,* a novel in
which subjective imagination dominated apparently for the first
time in Robbe-Grillet's work. (*Un Régicide,* which also showed
this interest in imagination, was not published until 1978; thus,
for his critics *La Jalousie* represented a break with Robbe-Grillet's
previous works although for Robbe-Grillet this subjective aspect
was the continuation of a permanent interest which only surfaced
again nearly ten years after the first novel.) *La Jalousie* sold only
600 copies in its first year despite the fact that Robbe-Grillet's
reputation as a novelist was spreading. Once again Robbe-Grillet
had given his readers something they were not yet prepared for.

The Theoretical Work

The negative reactions or the critical silence which greeted *La
Jalousie* inspired Robbe-Grillet's reflections on the nature of the
novel. He had published book reviews beginning as early as 1951
in *Critique* and in the *Nouvelle Nouvelle Revue Française* focusing
on works that suited his taste, those with " 'structured' plots,
fictional puzzles, and complicated actions. . . ."[5] He had en-

joyed, for example, Graham Greene's *Brighton Rock* and James M. Cain's *The Postman Always Rings Twice*. (Other works which Robbe-Grillet cites as having influenced his views on the novel are Kafka's *The Castle*, Lewis Carroll's *Alice in Wonderland*, Sartre's *La Nausée*, Camus's *L'Etranger*, Raymond Queneau's *Le Chiendent*, Raymond Roussel's *Impressions d'Afrique*, Faulkner's *Sanctuary*, and the works of Maurice Blanchot.) In 1955 the then daily news magazine *L'Express* asked him to explain his theoretical position in a series of nine articles to be published once every two weeks under the rubric "La Littérature aujourd'hui." The combative and somewhat defiant tone of the articles as well as the purposeful simplicity of the ideas they expressed won the indignant attention of the general reading public.

Robbe-Grillet was then asked by Jean Paulhan to expand these ideas for the more specialized literary and intellectual public of the *Nouvelle Nouvelle Revue Française;* another series of five essays appeared in *France-Observateur* in 1956. These articles were seen as constituting a kind of manifesto and in the minds of critics and readers Robbe-Grillet became the chief theoretician of this experimental literature. Several of these articles and essays were then revised and collected into Robbe-Grillet's only theoretical volume, *Pour un nouveau roman,* which appeared in 1963. Thus, contrary to what some of his detractors supposed, this engineer with no background in literature did not begin writing by attempting to change literature into science. Robbe-Grillet was a practitioner of the novel first and became a theoretician of the novel only when he realized to his surprise and bemusement that there existed a correct, and what is more, a natural way to tell a story and that his novels broke ancient and sacred rules of literary invention.

With an increasingly cogent grasp of the philosophical, moral, and political implications of his own writing and in defense of himself and the Nouveau Roman against attacks accusing his novels of sterility and inhumanity and suggesting that he return to writing statistical articles on the cattle population in France and leave literature to those who knew how to write, Robbe-Grillet developed the outlines of theories to explain the New

Novel to a reading public still looking to the nineteenth century for answers to twentieth-century issues. Expressing his distress at being considered a difficult writer and explaining his original expectation of appealing to a mass audience and not merely an audience of specialists, he began *Pour un nouveau roman* with the disclaimer that he was not a theoretician but that he wrote theoretical articles hoping to clear up the misunderstanding between himself and the public.

Hostile critics expended a great deal of energy in those days pointing out discrepancies between Robbe-Grillet's theories and his actual work and between his theoretical pronouncements from one article to the next. One reason for the apparent discrepancies is that critics sometimes focused on single aspects of his explanations and thereby distorted them or gave certain ideas undue emphasis. When Robbe-Grillet attempted to restore proper balance to the interpretation of his thought by supporting aspects not taken up by the critics, he was accused of having changed his mind. On the other hand his theories took shape as he wrote novels, and when he later found that no sooner had he theorized on his fiction than he was tempted to write his next work of fiction in challenge to his theory, he was pleased at the dialectical relationship between the two in his own mind. Thus, as Robbe-Grillet points out, at the very time that he was writing *La Jalousie,* he was condemning the use of metaphor in his theoretical work, and yet *La Jalousie* is full of metaphors, beginning with its very title. His basic continuity is his intention to create new forms, to experiment, and to challenge any system which has become or is on its way toward becoming sanctified.

Several principal points characterized Robbe-Grillet's thought on literature in the 1950s and have remained as the foundation for his theory and fiction since then. Although the names of Husserl, Heidegger, or Merleau-Ponty rarely appear in his work, Robbe-Grillet had clearly absorbed certain tenets of phenomenology: the world was neither significant nor absurd, objects were neither symbolic nor meaningless; the world, objects, man simply existed, together in the same space and time. Thus, the world need produce neither anguish nor nausea in man; it hides nothing.

In "Une Voie pour le roman futur" (1956) Robbe-Grillet urges that objects be allowed to exist for their own sakes and not merely as permanent supports for man's assignation of meaning. If they carry meaning, it is only a temporary meaning, such as the temporary significance which comes to be associated with the figure-8 shapes or the half-smoked cigarettes in *Le Voyeur,* published the year before. Robbe-Grillet predicted the discomfort writers would feel, were already feeling, with adjectives that reached for the romantic hidden heart of the world where its secrets lay; writers would no longer dig into the world but rather would look at its surface, measure it, define it in its own terms, not in anthropomorphic terms.

In 1957 in his article "Sur quelques notions perimées," Robbe-Grillet discusses the problems of character, story line, political commitment, and the separation of form and content and tries to present a new way of looking at these issues. He notes that characters in the novels of the nineteenth century had names, psychological traits, histories, social standing, while more modern novelists rejected these limitations and created characters without names, with minimal names, or with only initials thus undermining the notion of a character as a unique and solid presence in the world. Kafka's K, for example, has no relations, no past; Faulkner had given two characters the same name; Beckett's characters are reduced to mere voices. In the traditional novel the reader and writer both pretend they are dealing with a real person and a real story. The author guarantees the reality of what he writes; he is God and knows the outcome of the story and the unconscious passions of all his "real" characters. The author is the reassuring guarantee that truth does exist since he holds it in his possession. The world is explainable.

But unlike the traditional writer, directed by his genius like a seer directed by his gods, modern writers do not know a truth which they might transmit to their readers. The only truth is the work itself. Just as the plots of these modern novels cannot be summarized, no truth can be separated, extracted out, and digested. In the same article Robbe-Grillet also discusses the problem of political commitment in art, pointing out that the existing revolutionary countries could not tolerate modern art because they too held a truth which it was the duty of art to express. But modern authors, according to Robbe-Grillet, can be faithful only to the necessities of their art. Art is inefficient in provoking improvements or upheavals in society, and a novel with a political position to push is better written as nonfiction, as a tract. These opinions won Robbe-Grillet the criticism that he was not concerned with the world around him or that perhaps he saw no problems in the world. Such an understanding based on willful misreading of his statements led to surprise in 1960 when Robbe-Grillet's name appeared among the names of those who signed the *Manifeste des 121,* a public statement of support for the Algerians in their war of independence against France and a statement of disagreement with the French government's colonialist policies.

But Robbe-Grillet has maintained throughout his career that as a *writer of fiction* the only revolution he feels he can bring about is a revolution in the domain of literature. The need to revolutionize literature in the 1950s was urgent, for the literature of Balzac, which had grown out of the era of the rise of the bourgeoisie, was irrelevant to a world which no longer had faith in the dictatorship of the bourgeoisie, with its accompanying alienation in the name of the accumulation of wealth and power and with its aura of rightful, natural ownership.

Claiming that he was constantly taken aback by the reactions to his work, Robbe-Grillet wrote another article in 1958 in response to the poor reception accorded *La Jalousie* in 1957 and the continued accusation that his novels not merely dethroned man but tried to obliterate anything human. In "Nature, humanisme, tragédie" Robbe-Grillet skillfully argues that the false complicity with nature that was the foundation of nineteenth-century literature was a surreptitious acceptance of tragedy and of a fixed condition of mankind in the world based on the notion of human nature as permanent, static, and known. Far from clinging to an impossible cold objectivity that posits man as no different from the world around him, *La Jalousie* in fact concentrates on nothing but man in the most subjective way possible.

It is a novel in which nothing exists but as seen through a man's eyes or distorted through his imagination. What Robbe-Grillet hoped to obliterate with *La Jalousie,* however, was the notion that this "human nature" was predetermined, defined in advance; rather, man's nature is in a constant state of becoming, as he experiences that world around him and as this contact filters through his own particular mental processing system.

This claim of complete subjectivity was proof to some critics that Robbe-Grillet had reversed his previous untenable theoretical position based on the desire to see the world as object and not to invest it with man's murky superstitions and cultural prejudices. But Robbe-Grillet had never tried to maintain that objects did not become temporarily invested with meaning, only that that meaning did not exist without man, that objects in themselves carried no hidden significance. No one sees the world as it is; rather, as the phenomenologists say, consciousness of an object is always intentional; the object is always restructured by the perceiving mind. It is the implications of the notion of a hidden correspondence between man and the world around him that cause Robbe-Grillet's rejection in "Nature, humanisme, tragédie" of metephor. Metaphorical language by its very nature presupposes a basic unity among things because it is upon this similarity that the metaphor is built. Nevertheless, Robbe-Grillet's objection is not to the use of metaphor but rather to the idea that the similarities between things implied in the metaphor exist without man.

Most likely the new emphasis on subjectivity in Robbe-Grillet's explanations of his work came in part as a result of the analyses of his work done by American professor Bruce Morrissette. Articles on Robbe-Grillet by Morrissette began appearing in 1958, and in 1963 he published the first book-length study of Robbe-Grillet's work in both novel and film. This study was in fact published by Les Editions de Minuit and included an introduction by Roland Barthes expressing his disagreement with Morrissette's interpretation and developing the thesis that there were two Robbe-Grillets: Barthes's own modern Robbe-Grillet, interested in surface descriptions and manipulation of literary structures, and Morrissette's more traditional Robbe-Grillet, still devoted, perhaps in spite of himself, to humanistic and metaphysical concerns. That Robbe-Grillet would enjoy the confrontation of these two points of view is not surprising; that he was influenced by Morrissette's interpretations, as he had been by Barthes's, is clear from the new slant in his theoretical writing of the period toward an explanation of the fiction as highly subjective. This is not to say that such a slant falsified his previous discussions of his own work; although that subjectivity had always existed in the works, up to that point Robbe-Grillet was less interested in writing about that aspect of the books, an inherently less controversial one. The addition of Barthes's contestatory preface to Morrissette's analysis signals that Robbe-Grillet did not consider these points of view correct, incorrect, or mutually exclusive. They existed side by side. His willingness to accept interpretations despite their distance from his own conscious intentions is an attitude which has remained with Robbe-Grillet throughout his career.

Thus, Robbe-Grillet's defense of the Nouveau Roman in his theoretical work shifted; he now saw his fiction as concerned primarily with the perception of the world by a consciousness which was anything but dispassionate and impartial. Instead Robbe-Grillet emphasized the extremely passionate or emotional nature of the consciousness, for example, in *Le Voyeur,* a sexually obsessed psychotic, in *La Jalousie,* an irrationally jealous husband, in *Dans le labyrinthe,* a sick, delirious, hallucinating soldier. As late as 1966 in a lecture delivered in Hungary Robbe-Grillet underlined the highly subjective nature of the descriptions in his New Novels.[6]

In "Nouveau Roman, homme nouveau," written in 1961, Robbe-Grillet began to speak more systematically of the notion that there is no reality preexisting the text. He had been struck by this fact while he was writing the description of the seagulls in *Le Voyeur* and found that he was neither reproducing a true picture of a seagull nor interested in doing so. In "Nouveau Roman, homme nouveau" he stresses the new relationship between the writer and his work. The writer does not write because he has a statement about the world which he would like to make.

Rather his writing is more like a search for that statement; the statement does not exist before the work; the statement is the work itself. Since then Robbe-Grillet has often expressed his need, not to reveal to the world a truth hidden inside him, but to construct, to manipulate the world outside him according to his desire. It is also in this essay that Robbe-Grillet expresses his rather unrequited solidarity with the nonspecialist in literature in whom Robbe-Grillet places his hopes; the uninitiated reader will eventually become the *homme nouveau* because he is, as the young Robbe-Grillet was, free of literary prejudices and habits and will be able to recognize in the world of Robbe-Grillet's novels a reflection of his own world, not a novelistic world in which events are chronological, casual, and comprehensible. Robbe-Grillet makes the same point in his introduction to the *ciné-roman* of *L'Année dernière à Marienbad* from the same year. If the spectator frees himself from the prejudices inculcated into him by out-of-date, outworn world views of the nineteenth century, he will agree that the world he sees on the screen in *L'Année dernière à Marienbad* is most realistic.

The Nouveau Nouveau Roman

By this time the opportunity to work on films had presented itself and Robbe-Grillet temporarily put the novel aside. It was also at this time that new shifts in the theory and practice of the New Novelists and their supporters began to occur, led by articles by such people as Philippe Sollers and Jean Ricardou. Once again open to outside influences, Robbe-Grillet began emphasizing new concerns in his writing. He moved away from the objective/subjective quarrel toward a more fruitful stance. It was no longer reality or irreality as a pair that interested him, but rather anything false; that is, it was the fiction itself which now received attention. He began to express more clearly the role of description in his works, abandoning his stress on the ideas either that geometrical precision would cleanse the world of the sliminess of man's interpretations or later that an object's very size, form, and number can vary depending on the tension experienced by the perceiver of the object. In this changed critical climate there emerged increased emphasis on the idea of construction, of literary creation as work.

Thus, in his articles dating from this period Robbe-Grillet shows a deeper awareness of the fact that his descriptions are radically different from any objects; they are constructions made of words. As Ricardou points out, the longer the description, the more precise and detailed, the less real the object seems and the farther away from any normal perspective it moves. Robbe-Grillet notes in "Temps et description dans le récit d'aujourd'hui" that the descriptions in a book are the book; that is, if a reader skips the pages of description, as he might in a Balzac book, in which the description of objects is redundant because it merely serves to reemphasize some aspect of a character's personality or social condition, in a New Novel the reader will come to the last page, having skipped the entire book. Furthermore, contrary to the procedures of a Balzac, all geared toward making the reader accept and believe the idea that when he reads a description of a person that person is real, Robbe-Grillet increasingly began to emphasize the fictionality of his objects, his characters, his scenes. The new emphasis was already apparent in Robbe-Grillet's films in the stilted style of Robbe-Grillet's actors, much criticized for bad acting, i.e., for not seeming like real people.

With his new understanding of the role of fiction in mind, in the early 1960s Robbe-Grillet redirected his interpretation of his books written up to that point and of the novels to be written thereafter. In a 1963 updated version of the article "Du réalisme à la réalité," which had originally appeared in 1955, Robbe-Grillet states that although he had agreed to interpretations centered on the subjectivity of his works, he also realized that this subjectivity and the earlier emphasis on objectivity were never really at the core of what he felt he was doing and what he wanted to do. He did not want to reproduce in his writing a preexisting "objectal" reality any more than he wanted to express his philosophy of life, his insights into human nature, or his political convictions. He wrote because he wanted to construct, to create forms. Along with this deepened insight into his own intentions came a sharper picture of the role of his audience and readers.

The reader was now more insistently than ever asked to participate in the creation of the fiction by actively working at perceiving the construction the reader himself was engaged in while reading. The ludic aspects of literary creation began to be frequently discussed as man's best opportunity to exercise his freedom. In 1970 Robbe-Grillet was asked by the publisher Skira to do a volume for their series "Sentiers de la création" in which he would explain his approach to the creation of a piece of art, in this case his film *L'Eden et après*. Unfortunately other interests took precedence and the book was never completed.

At this same time a group of young writers, among them Sollers, Ricardou, Jean-Pierre Faye, Julia Kristeva, and Denis Roche, began publishing the journal *Tel Quel* (1960). Robbe-Grillet's association and involvement with this group coincides with the end of the first major phase of his work, and eventually Robbe-Grillet's writing and the writing of the members of this group came to be called the Nouveau Nouveau Roman and to be characterized by increased emphasis on generative structures, on writing as extremely conscious manipulation of narrative forms. The Tels Quelists, particularly Sollers, were in some ways disciples of Robbe-Grillet, interested in leaving outmoded literary conventions behind and engaging in a literature of experimentation. Their increasingly extreme leftist political orientation, however, eventually resulted in their excommunication of Robbe-Grillet, who in a sense had been their progenitor, but who continued to refuse commitment to anything but literature.

Partly because of his increased visibility as a filmmaker, the intelligence and the polemical tone of his theoretical work, and the violence of his detractors and supporters, but mainly because of his outgoing nature, sense of humor, and ability to express himself lucidly and entertainingly, Robbe-Grillet continues to be sought out by educational, cultural, and literary groups in France and all over the world as a speaker. After the publication of *Pour un nouveau roman,* Robbe-Grillet wrote fewer theoretical articles but gave numerous interviews and lectures instead. In the 1960s and 1970s he appeared at writers' conferences in Belgrade, Tokyo, Athens, and Leningrad (where his work was criticized as an example of bourgeois decadence). He has been invited to the United States on several occasions to teach courses on film and on the novel in California and New York; one of his biggest reading publics in fact is the student in the American university, where his works are read alongside the plays of Racine. His novels have been translated into twenty-five foreign languages and as of 1971 his books had sold 430,000 copies in France alone. Robbe-Grillet is at this time one of the extremely small number of writers in France who would be able to live on the royalties from his books. In 1971 a conference on the Nouveau Roman took place at the International Cultural Center at Cerisy-la-Salle in France and in 1975 a similar conference was devoted entirely to the works of Robbe-Grillet.

Although Robbe-Grillet exaggerates to some extent the re-sistance to the new approach to literature of which he was the major spokesman in the 1950s, there are striking examples to support his contention. Whereas in the year *La Jalousie* appeared in France it sold 600 copies and was judged to be unreadable, it has now become not only readable but a classic; with its clear, correct French, its relatively simple vocabulary, and its repetitions of scenes, it is even used successfully as a reader to teach French. It has traveled quite a distance from unreadability. It is further true, as Robbe-Grillet frequently points out, that as his works appeared they were criticized in the name of the excellence of the preceding works. In some way this is no doubt gratifying to Robbe-Grillet; as long as his most recent work provokes criticism, he is not repeating himself. His works may become classics, absorbed into the literary mainstream, as the years pass, but the newest novel or film always represents, as Robbe-Grillet hopes, a departure from that classicism and a challenge to it.

Chapter Two
Les Gommes

From Robbe-Grillet's first published novel, *Les Gommes* (1953),[1] to *Souvenirs du triangle d'or* (1978) the novel form and Robbe-Grillet's use of the novel form have undergone basic changes. Many of the seeds of these changes were already present in *Les Gommes*, which became one of the first French novels to pose reading and writing as problematic. Robbe-Grillet's own awareness of what he was doing with the novel sharpened as he debated with critics and commentators of his work for twenty-five years. It stands to reason that *Les Gommes*, although it was considered fairly startling when it first appeared, is now the least radical of Robbe-Grillet's novels in its manipulation of narrative forms and is most easily recuperated, that is, stripped of its radicality, its strangeness, and reduced to a story that can be reconstructed and told.

In a northern European city the ninth in a series of seemingly politically motivated assassinations occurs, except that this time the intended victim, Daniel Dupont, is not killed but only slightly wounded. To forestall any attempt to complete the task, Dupont, who has close contacts with the Ministry of the Interior, allows everyone to believe he has been killed when in fact he is only hiding out at the clinic of a doctor acquaintance of his, Dr. Juard, until he can return to his study to gather up some important papers before leaving the city that same evening under police protection. In the meantime the Bureau of Investigation has dispatched a new special agent, Wallas, to investigate the crime. Having very little to go on, not even a corpse, Wallas spends the day attempting to gather clues from neighbors and acquaintances of Dupont. In the evening he decides to inspect the Dupont house coincidentally just at the moment that Dupont himself secretly returns to his study to collect his documents before leaving town. Thinking Dupont is the assassin returning to the scene of the crime, Wallas shoots and kills him exactly twenty-four hours after the original attempt occurred, duplicating the original assassin's plan. Thus, *Les Gommes* might be a fairly standard detective story with an ironic twist at the end when the detective sent to investigate the crime turns out to be himself the murderer.

The Problem of Predestination

But in *Les Gommes* Robbe-Grillet refuses to deal with the psychology, the humanity, the personality, of his characters and instead spends many pages indifferently, flatly describing the surfaces of objects which refuse to be symbolic, refuse to exist only for the sake of man, and instead claim the right to exist for themselves. But man has a difficult time accepting this *être-là des choses* and insists on interpreting this existence as signs to himself, pointing to his destiny. Robbe-Grillet explores the idea of predestination in *Les Gommes* by using the myth of Oedipus. In his discussion of *Les Gommes* Bruce Morrissette lets no reference to Oedipus escape his attention and his very thorough reading is a careful recuperation of this modern use of an ancient myth.[2] But the reader who has learned to interpret the meaning of objects in literature in this way is condemned always to find the same meaning—man and his fate. "The Sphinx is before me; it questions me; I need not even attempt to understand the terms of the enigma it puts to me; there is only one possible answer, a single answer to everything: man."[3] Robbe-Grillet uses the references he makes to Oedipus to deny, not to substantiate, the validity of the idea of predestination. As Olga Bernal suggests, the references to Oedipus are glimpses of the trap Robbe-Grillet does not want the reader to fall into.[4]

Like the traditional reader Wallas is a detective; it is his job to look at objects and to see in them motives, actions, clues, meanings. As he walks down the street his detective eye scans the passers-by and he penetrates their experiences by postulating the lives hidden behind the exteriors: "A little farther, a gentleman in a black overcoat and hat comes out of a house and passes him; middle aged, comfortable, frequent stomach trouble . . ." (47). "At one intersection Wallas notices opposite him the dispeptic gentleman he has seen before, crossing the street. He doesn't look any better after having eaten breakfast; perhaps it is worry and not stomach trouble that gives him that expression. . . . He is wearing black: he is going to the post office to send a telegram announcing someone's death" (54). Wallas's construction of a life inside the "black overcoat" is innocent enough but the tendency toward this type of reconstruction leads Wallas to register and ultimately to act upon the suggestions offered by the references to Oedipus. In a sense Wallas assumes the destiny of Oedipus because he believes objects must be interpreted, that is, must be made to render up their real meanings, all of which ultimately point to Wallas, the innocent, somewhat naive detective, as the assassin. Wallas kills Dupont because he refuses to recognize the fact that a myth can only exist if someone believes in it. In the same way the Oedipus traps are set for the reader as well, who, if he falls into them, has before him a rather entertaining, odd, but basically traditional and comprehensible detective story; this reader has neglected all the radical aspects of the book and a good bit of its humor and irony. Furthermore, this reader has no way of explaining certain aspects of the book and must therefore ignore them: for example, the long description of objects with no connection to the myth, like the slices of tomato or a piece of ham on Dupont's dinner plate.

Les Gommes then provides many elements permitting a reading based on the myth of Oedipus, yet, although *Les Gommes* is available for such a reading, there is at the same time something twisted in this modern version of Oedipus that signals to the reader that the text is not only a modern version of Oedipus, that in fact the function of the myth of Oedipus in *Les Gommes* is to permit the author to make ironic comments on the tradition of allowing elements in a text to be defined in relation to a structure outside the book. Wallas had been to this city as a child once before; he says he and his mother had come to see a female relative. Later in the book, as the symbolic evidence mounts against him, Wallas claims he now "remembers" that he and his mother had not come to see a female relative at all; they had come in search of Wallas's father. When Wallas "remembers" this essential clue, he has finally swallowed the bait and taken for sincerity the ironic references to Oedipus. The text comments, "How could he have forgotten it?" (231) and that, of course, is precisely the question. He has not in fact called back into his conscious mind the memory of a scene he had once experienced; rather, he creates for himself a false memory to help him grasp a situation in the present which he cannot explain: who killed Dupont? We are warned not to be misled by the references to a system extrinsic to the text in the first description of the Greek sculpture on the central town square; the Greeks in the sculpture are described as "probably symbolic" (58). Such an aside to the audience departs from the fictional code of the twentieth century and resembles comments made directly to the audience by Fielding in *Tom Jones* or Thackeray in *Barry Lyndon*. Ironic asides here are meant to distance the reader from the text and prevent him from falling into the trap of judging a fictional text with reference to a system extrinsic to the text.

Thus, the text undermines the possibility of a symbolic reading by mocking such a reading and creating a distance between the reader and the events and characters he is reading about. What the text explores is the possibility of a superficial reading; by juxtaposing objects, surfaces, and perceptions to interpretations, meaning, and reasoning Robbe-Grillet demonstrates the chasm permanently separating perception and meaning and the arbitrary nature of the connection between them.

The Problem of Meaning

Like a Greek tragedy *Les Gommes* is organized into five chapters plus a prologue and an epilogue.[5] The events which occur in *Les Gommes* take place within a period of twenty-four hours, but it is a special period, a time of fiction, when time is out of phase with itself, unpredictable. During these twenty-four problematic fictional hours the normal link between perception and meaning is also disturbed such that communication among the characters breaks down. Messages are untransmitted, incorrectly transmitted, or incorrectly interpreted; sounds fail to communicate their messages. Wallas unsuccessfully tries to decipher the hushed conversations of other people. Announcements made over the loudspeaker at the train station are incomprehensible. Clearly, an attempt at communication is being made, but "the original message is lost—transformed into a gigantic oracle, magnificent, indecipherable, and terrifying" (200). The message, as if from an oracle, is perceived, but its meaning cannot be grasped; the split between perception and meaning widens.

Written attempts to communicate fare no better than attempts at oral communication. Failures to communicate, thwarted attempts to extract meaning from messages, reading and writing as problematic activities in *Les Gommes* can all be thought of as models of these same problems encountered in the process of reading or writing fiction. In nearly every instance of writing mentioned there is something missing, something unclear, or something misinterpreted. Letters are missing in Wallas's memory of the perfect eraser he is seeking; only *Oe* and *pe* remain, with the center two letters *di* lost. Wallas and Laurent intercept a note in which one word and possibly another phrase are illegible, but they must discover the message hidden behind the words of the note. One word resembles " 'ellipse' or 'eclipse' or . . . could be 'align' or 'idem' or a lot of other things" (161). For Laurent and Wallas the note must be a transmitter of meaning. If the meaning of a word or a phrase is multiple, communication has broken down and truth, the goal of a good detective, is obscured.[6]

The note is not meaningless; it suffers from an excess of meaning. An excess of signs in the story puts a halt to interpretation just as well. In the train station the ads, announcements, posters, each screaming its message, clash with one another, overload Wallas's ability to take them all in and thus become undecipherable; their meanings reverberate against each other, multiply, void, and echo other meanings so that finally the message is lost. The text, the signs insist on their own presence. Although the posters read: "Citizens Awake! Citizens Awake! Citizens Awake!" (48), they attract only the attention of an old man passing by

who carefully deciphers the print "from the beginning all the
way to the end, steps back to consider the whole poster with a
shrug, . . . then goes on his way in some perplexity, wondering
if he has not missed the point" (48–49); the old man's perplexity
is a reflection of that of the traditional reader attempting and
inevitably failing to penetrate beyond the text to its insights into
local color, metaphysics, psychology, mythology, or a number
of other methods of systematizing meaning.

In a sense the traditional reader already has in his mind the
Ur-text of the novel written in these different patterns, and the
duty of the author of a novel, a duty Robbe-Grillet both complies
with and refuses in this novel, is to write a text whose meaning
conforms to one of those models, in other words, to create a text
which is already finished. Thus, when Wallas visits the Dupont
study and finds the piece of paper with the unfinished sentence,
"which cannot prevent" (90), as a good traditional reader, he
cannot resist completing the text: " 'which cannot prevent
. . .'—'. . . death . . .' obviously. That is the word he was
looking for when he went downstairs to eat" (90). An incomplete
text, i.e., one whose meaning does not conform to a preexistent
model, is intolerable. In some sense the impasse the novel had
reached by the early 1950s rested on the same dilemma: signs
and the order of signs had to be reproduced according to a prees-
tablished nineteenth-century model. Although it is not clear that
at this time Robbe-Grillet was fully aware of the challenge he
was making to traditional literature with *Les Gommes*, posing
reading and writing as a problem was to become one of the major
themes in his later work and in the work of other New Novelists.

Although the written word is problematic in *Les Gommes*, it
nevertheless carries inordinate weight with the characters. The
newspaper, for example, is brought up several times: "Don't you
read the papers?" several characters ask in surprise. The newspaper
represents a translation into writing of reality—even more, of
truth itself. Thus, the café owner and his client Antoine consult
the newspaper to settle their argument about whether the name
of the attack victim was Albert or Daniel Dupont and about

whether or not he actually died. Bona, the mastermind of the political assassinations, learns of the supposed success of his agent Garinati's mission by consulting the newspaper and furthermore convinces Garinati, who knows very well he had failed in his mission, of the error in his own experience and memory. The past is unstable and can be rearranged by a new version of the past written down, and ultimately, the newspaper is correct; Dupont is dead by the end of the book. In some sense the characters' belief in the truth of the writing of which they themselves are made is justified: in fiction there is no truth other than the writing itself; extrinsic reality cannot correct what is written because reality and what is written operate in two separate spheres. It becomes Robbe-Grillet's position that literature is not a copy of reality but an independent fabrication of a network of signs that indicate each other.

Robbe-Grillet's consciousness of the difficulty of transforming modes of reading emerges in comments made by Police Chief Laurent on a report written by one of the policemen. Forming part of the stream of metacommentary in *Les Gommes*, Laurent's remarks can also be read as pertinent to Robbe-Grillet as an author, predicting reactions of a reader, perhaps an editor, of *Les Gommes:* "This boy is a little young, of course: you can tell it's his first crime. . . . The enthusiasm of a neophyte, you understand" (190). In further metacommentary Wallas becomes the reader, reviewing and resuming the progress of the novel up to a certain point. "The first pages discuss in detail, but without digressions or commentary, the telephone call from Doctor Juard. . . . Then comes an extremely precise description of the house and its environs. . . . Then follow the police observations proper . . ." (190–91). "It is apparent that the author only reproduces all these trifling remarks out of a concern for objectivity . . ." (192). The police report is written in a pastiche of Robbe-Grillet's style, describing the exact size and weight of seemingly unimportant objects, details termed with an edge of self-mockery "exaggeratedly detailed notations" (191).

The Problem of Reason

As Wallas reads the police officer's summary of the day's events and with it the summary of his own actions, he absorbs specifications for his own role in the remainder of the text. Like Garinati, who must memorize Bona's plan of action, his stage directions, before he attempts to murder Dupont, Wallas too needs to act according to a fixed plan, orders from someone outside him. But for Wallas this need is particularly urgent because he is different from everyone else. He is a stranger in town, a mere roomer among the allies at the Café des Alliés; he is not dressed like the people around him; and worst, his forehead is, according to Fabius, the respected head of the Bureau of Investigation, too small for him to be a special agent. Wallas must work to resemble those around him in order not to disappoint them. In several scenes in which he allows his doubts about his own nature or identity to cause him to lie or to seem guilty, he resembles Henri Michaux's Plume, born guilty, or Inspector Clouseau of the French *Surêté*. Like the eraser he is searching for, his character is soft, malleable, allowing him to become anyone, including, eventually, the assassin.

Wallas judges himself by a personal standard of truth and constantly finds himself not measuring up to the standard. In his conversations with the woman on the street and with Anna, Dupont's housekeeper, he continuously compares his statements to them with some internal blueprint or plan of how the conversation should be going. This blueprint corresponds to what Wallas feels is the truth. Unfortunately the other characters do not always carry the same blueprints and therefore Wallas is unable to anticipate people's reactions to him. When he speaks to Mme Jean, the woman sweeping the street, she refuses to respond correctly. When he asks for the central post office, she asks, "What do you mean, the central post office?" (50). By the end of their conversation Wallas has invented a story about a relative of his who has died; Wallas has been forced to lie to excuse himself for having asked directions to the post office. Wallas gradually takes onto himself an increasing burden of guilt about things which trouble no one else and he insists upon the existence of an absolute truth which no one else recognizes. At the same time Wallas tries so hard to conform to what he perceives as the truth of who he is and how he should behave that when he wants to prove his identity to the café owner, he realizes that he does not resemble his own identity picture. Only after the murder, once he has made the ultimate concession to the wills of others and has killed Dupont, is he able to recognize himself again in his ID picture. He finally corresponds with himself because he has fulfilled the desire of everyone around him for a solution to the murder, accommodatingly providing both corpse and killer, and fulfilling the prophecy he himself wrote out by completing Dupont's last words to read: " 'which cannot prevent . . .'—'. . . death . . .' obviously." After Dupont's murder, life falls back into place. Time corresponds with itself again. Wallas, the agitating element which forced time out of its even path, has now been absorbed into the rigid and perfectly operating mechanism of everyone else's plans.[7]

Well-organized plans are the result of reasoning, a mode of thought useful for both detectives and criminals. Wallas and Laurent hope to come to the truth (". . . the truth . . . the truth . . . the truth . . ." [198]) through logic. There are nine murders on nine successive nights, all committed at the same hour; following Wallas's logic, they must be connected. Wallas has come from out of town, takes a room near the scene of the crime, has a revolver from which one bullet has been shot and which is the same kind of gun Dupont had; according to Laurent's logic, Wallas may well be the murderer. The minds of the characters in *Les Gommes* constantly churn, searching for reasons behind actions, looking for connections among events. Little of this mental activity, however, leads to positive results. Mme Dupont divorced her husband because he based all actions on reasoned, logical decisions. "I had nothing but virtues to reproach him for, really: never doing anything without thinking first, never changing his mind, never being wrong" (175). For Wallas the result of all his reasoning is to lead him directly to committing the crime. Some fault, some major flaw in the very process of reasoning in order to find truth guarantees that following his reason is the surest way not to reach the goal he seeks. He searches for the phantom of truth in the labyrinths of the city, refusing to recognize that there is no truth, thus forever doomed to frustration. Like the work done at the post office, described by Mme Jean, which is ". . . subject to certain secret regulations and [which] engendered a number of rituals that were generally incomprehensible" (184), Wallas is engaged in a task "both complicated and futile" (184).

Wallas's faith in logic is unjustified; logic and reason are deceptive. Reconstructing the invisible lines that hold causes and effects together leads Wallas to murder and leads other characters to madness, a recurrent theme in *Les Gommes*. When Laurent hears that his superiors suspect the recent flurry of crimes of being politically motivated, he considers this type of reasoning worthy of the "old lunatic" (72), Roy-Dauzet, Minister of the Interior. The great detective, Fabius, famed within his department in particular for his great success in solving crimes, also seems to have suffered from his many years of piecing together evidence and separating the strands of knotty enigmas. Certain peculiar "inexplicable obstinacies" (56) like measuring the foreheads of his agents and insisting on the importance of disguises are more humorous than incapacitating: "The caricature, famous in the Bureau of Investigation and in the whole Ministry, represents Fabius disguised as an 'idler': hat pulled down over his eyes, huge dark glasses, and an outrageously false beard hanging to the ground; bent double, this creature prowls 'discreetly' through the countryside, among the startled cows and horses" (56). There is a more serious charge, however: "Already people were saying that he mistrusted easy solutions, now it is whispered that he had ceased to believe in the existence of any solution whatever" (56). An unacceptable attitude, no doubt, for a detective, but exactly the one Robbe-Grillet counsels the reader to adopt, forces him to adopt when dealing with his works.

The most interesting madness explored in *Les Gommes* is in the character of Bona. In the only scene in which he appears, he sits waiting for Garinati, gazing out the window over the rooftops of the city. The description of these rooftops, seen like a painting

through the frame of the window, suggests certain authorial
concerns with the nature of the relationship between reality and
art. In this sense Bona is assimilated to the creator, to Robbe-
Grillet himself. Furthermore, it is Bona's scenario that Garinati
must follow in the assassination attempt and in this respect Bona
is a controlling force directing the activity of all the characters
in the book. He is in fact what Robbe-Grillet calls one of his
"organizational poles . . . which organize or claim to organize
the whole narrative."[8] He has the scenario for the rest of the book
planned; since Garinati has failed to kill Dupont, another assassin
will appear, Bona correctly predicts, and will succeed: "Nothing
can keep his plan from being carried out" (120). Because the
book is his plan, Bona knows all and sees all: "Bona always
knows" (34). If he at first seems to be mistaken about Dupont
and his death, it is only the appearance of an error on his part,
a shortsighted view; Bona is proven correct. But there is a certain
maniacal quality about him; the assassinations he plans must take
place at exactly the time and in exactly the way he has specified,
flawlessly. He awaits Garinati in a room divested of any of the
accoutrements of a normal apartment except for two lawn chairs
and, oddly enough, new tapestries on the walls, as if in some
madman's throne room. The king is dressed with care. "Bona is
not dressed for sitting indoors. His overcoat is tightly buttoned
up to the collar, his hands are gloved, and he keeps his hat on.
He is waiting, motionless on this uncomfortable chair, bolt up-
right, his hands crossed on his knees, his feet riveted to the floor,
betraying no impatience. He is looking straight ahead at the
little spots left by the raindrops on the windowpanes . . ." (95).
Bona has certain qualities of the evil genius fabricating mad
schemes like *Les Gommes*. He is the one who puts order in the
narrative and who at the same time incorporates disorder, crime,
insanity, like the figure of King Boris, the mad sovereign, which
Robbe-Grillet finds intriguing.[9] The king's word is the law, the
king embodies law and therefore truth and reason, and yet, the
king himself is a mad criminal.

Objects

Certain elements of *Les Gommes*, however, caused much greater trouble than even the mad king, Boris/Bona. Robbe-Grillet treats objects described in *Les Gommes* in a way in which they could not be treated in a traditional detective story. One of the most difficult sections of *Les Gommes* to assimilate into the story is a long description of a slice of tomato on Wallas's plate. "A quarter of tomato that is quite faultless, cut up by the machine into a perfectly symmetrical fruit. The peripheral flesh, compact, homogeneous, and a splendid chemical red, is of an even thickness between a strip of gleaming skin and the hollow where the yellow, graduated seeds appear in a row, kept in place by a thin layer of greenish jelly along a swelling of the heart" (152–53), and so on. When *Les Gommes* appeared, traditional criticism had no apparatus to deal with such a description, gratuitous, geometrical, unemotional; there was no way to integrate this description into the novel. The tomato slice is simply there, an example of *"l'être-là des choses."*

The erasers in the title proved a problem as well. In traditional literature the title of the book and the text it heads stand in a particular codified relationship to each other; namely, one is basically a repetition of the other. The title is a résumé of the text unifying it into a few key words, and the text is a kind of elaboration of the title. "If the title is a machine which erases its text, the text on the other hand is a machine which reads its title."[10] The problem with a title like *Les Gommes* is that although erasers are mentioned in the text, their connection to the story is problematic. Certainly this novel is not the story of some erasers in the way that *Anna Karenina* is the story of Anna Karenina or *L'Etranger* is the story of a stranger. In fact the erasers in the book are persistent attempts to erase the very story in which they appear, to deny the text which allows them to exist. Wallas pursues his hunt for the ideal eraser, for truth and logic, as if it were the Grail, in order to rub out the increasing number of ties that link him to the murder and that will eventually result in his accommodatingly providing the murder which allows the murder mystery to exist. Just before his final penetration into

the Dupont house where he commits the crime, Wallas makes
one last desperate attempt to find the eraser and replace the text
with an absence of text, with a void, the void between Monday
7:30 P.M. and Tuesday 7:30 P.M., when time was out of con-
junction with itself, so much so that twenty-four hours interpose
themselves between the time a bullet is fired and the time its
target is killed. The erasers are meant to eliminate those twenty-
four hours, to free Wallas from the weight of myths of meaning
which insist that behind phenomena there is meaning, that objects described in a text serve only to point the way to moral,
social, psychological, mythical systems outside language. These
systems direct Wallas toward the Dupont house: the Oedipus
myth, the resemblance between Wallas and the suspicious VS,
the coincidences of details, like the type of gun Wallas carries,
the insufficient breadth of his forehead, all trap him in a network
of meaning and doom him to completing the net around himself
just as he completed the sentence left unfinished on Dupont's
desk.

An object in *Les Gommes* much less heavily loaded than the
erasers, the paperweight in Dupont's study, provides a better
example of how Robbe-Grillet will use objects in later texts.
Compact, clean, dense, the form of the paperweight is a cube,
all sides equal, no extraneous parts; it is a perfect object, fitting
gracefully in the equally efficient life of Daniel Dupont and like
the eraser with very little a priori meaning attached to it. The
cube first appears early in the book in the scene in which Garinati
waits in the study for Dupont to return from dinner. Thereafter
any subsequent mention of objects with characteristics similar to
those of the cube call to mind this scene, the scene of an attempted
murder. Thus, when Wallas details the kind of eraser he wants,
a textual tie is created between the two objects; in a weak sense
the eraser and the cube are put into a metaphorical relationship
to each other for the structural attributes they share and for the
textual similarities that bring them into focus: "A kind of cube,
but slightly misshapen, a shiny block of gray lava, with its faces
polished as though by wear, the edges softened, compact, apparently hard, heavy as gold, looking about as big around as a

fist . . ." (21) and "a soft, crumbly gum eraser that friction does not twist but reduces to dust . . . a yellowish cube, about an inch or two long, with corners slightly rounded—maybe by use" (126). Once this metaphorical link is established, mention of one term of the metaphor inevitably calls up the other term. But once Wallas's last attempt to find the eraser he wants fails, he is left only with the paperweight and therefore with the murder scene. Significantly, the inoffensive paperweight with rounded edges transforms in the imagined scene with Dupont's imaginary son into "the heavy paperweight with sharp edges" (196) and in the final murder scene, under the deforming gaze of Wallas, it becomes menacing: "The cube of vitrified stone, with its sharp edges and deadly corners . . ." (236). No gaze is innocent, and as Olga Bernal points out, ". . . observation is a perturbation. The Robbe-Grilletian glance is characterized by its great transforming action."[11]

Early in Robbe-Grillet's career as a writer critics made the felicitous mistake of criticizing his writing by saying that the novels he wrote or the stories he told were not told in the natural, normal way which everyone recognizes as the right way. One of the theoretical bases of Robbe-Grillet's novels is that there is no natural, normal, right way to write fiction. The notion that the way to tell a story is natural fails to recognize the codification of any mode of communication, including fiction, and implies that the ability to understand a notation such as "many years later" comes naturally and is not learned. In *Les Gommes* Robbe-Grillet begins his twenty-five-year contestation of the idea of "nature," the nature of man, the nature of fiction, by systematically working against the codes of traditional narrative, by systematically breaking the rules of good writing. Traditional novels communicate a message the author wants to give the reader; the reader's job is to decipher the code, crack the nutshell of the writing to get to the meat of the message. But Robbe-Grillet's novels have no final meaning; the message is the process itself of reading. There is nothing to be extracted from the reading through the vehicle of transparent writing; the writing is stubbornly opaque. Perhaps the shape of the little tear on the back of the raincoat of one of the characters offers a key to what the reader is dealing with in *Les Gommes*: L, for *lecture, lire* ("reading"). Robbe-Grillet's early readers frequently referred to his use of geometrical terms and precisions to describe objects in his books; but his geometry is a special brand, all linear, two dimensional, and undirectional, the geometry of writing.

Chapter Three
Le Voyeur

Although *Les Gommes* broke with certain traditional narrative forms, in its use of descriptions, in the characterizations, in its manipulation of chronology, it was still an almost recuperable detective story. Critics of the book complained that the novelist had pointlessly complicated a simple story. Robbe-Grillet's reaction to such criticism was *Le Voyeur* (1955), a novel much more difficult to assimilate into the mainstream of novel tradition.[1] Like *Les Gommes*, *Le Voyeur* is constructed around a problematic murder. But the characterizations in *Le Voyeur* are far more limited; the role played by objects is even farther away from their traditional role in which objects are mere reflections of the characters in the action. The development of the plot is more disconcerting. Whereas in *Les Gommes* the murder which Wallas is investigating does not take place until the end, in *Le Voyeur* there is doubt that the murder took place at all.

Le Voyeur begins on a ferry. Mathias, a traveling watch salesman, is on his way to the island where he had lived as a child. His hope is that between the time he arrives on the island around 10 A.M. and the time the ferry leaves to return to the mainland at 4:15, he will be able to take advantage of his status as a former inhabitant of the island to gain people's confidence and sell, he hopes, perhaps even all his watches, ninety in all. As the boat is landing, Mathias calculates the exact amount of time he can give to the sale of each watch, four minutes, and still get back to the dock in time to catch the boat, for the next ferry off the island does not leave until Friday afternoon, four days later. As he stands on the deck, he notices a piece of cord wrapped in a figure 8 on the ground near him and picks it up. As he straightens, he notices a young girl standing against a post with her hands behind her back, staring at him. The boat docks, and Mathias arranges to rent a bicycle for his trip around the island and buys a pack of cigarettes and a bag of candy. His route will be a kind of figure 8, with the crossing point of the two loops just south of the port. His first stop is at the farm of Mme Leduc. Although he does not succeed in selling her a watch, he does hear from her about the problems she has been having with Jacqueline, the youngest of three daughters. Although only thirteen, Jacqueline has apparently already been involved in escapades with sexual overtones and other misadventures, including the break-up of at least one marriage engagement. At the very moment Mathias and Mme Leduc are talking, Jacqueline is guarding the family sheep a bit farther down the road, on a cliff overlooking the sea. After leaving Mme Leduc, Mathias sets off down the road toward the intersection of the main road and the path leading to the cliff where Jacqueline is watching the sheep. Part 1 of *Le Voyeur* ends here.

Since Part 2 begins on the right side of the page and Part 1 had ended on the right side, an entire blank page, page 88, separates Part 1 from Part 2. Part 2 begins with Mathias standing on the road next to his bicycle about forty-five minutes later just beyond the junction of the main road and the path leading to the cliffs. There he meets Mme Marek. Mathias has maintained a slight acquaintance with the Marek family and when he runs into old Mme Marek on the road he feels he must explain to her why he is standing all alone in the middle of the road. He tells her that he has just come from her farm, where he found no one, and was about to continue on his way when his bicycle started to give him trouble; just as she came up, he was fixing the chain. Mathias rides on and then stops in a café, where he learns that Jacqueline is missing and that her sister has been trying to find her. A man who seems to know Mathias comes into the bar and invites him to lunch with him and a young woman who lives with him; Mathias has no recollection of the man whatsoever. During lunch the "friend," Pierre or Jean Robin, angrily forbids his female companion ever again to visit her friend, Jacqueline. By the time Mathias leaves Robin's house, his time is beginning to run short and he hurriedly stops at the houses and towns along his circuit to try to sell as many watches as possible before the time for his departure from the island arrives. Just as he starts on the final stretch back to the port, his bicycle actually does start to give him trouble and in fact delays him so much that he misses his boat.

In Part 3, the next day, still on the island, Mathias awakens in a rented room. While he is having breakfast in the café, he learns that Jacqueline's body has been found. He suddenly remembers the three cigarette butts left on the cliff, and giving as an excuse that he wants to visit his old friends the Mareks, he sets off for the cliff. As he is looking in the grass for the cigarette butts, he notices someone else there, the woman companion of Jean Robin. She tells Mathias that she is sure that Robin killed Jacqueline; he disliked Jacqueline and had threatened her just the day before. Furthermore, the woman had found evidence that Robin has been on the cliff, a half-smoked cigarette. Mathias snatches this incriminating evidence from her and throws it into the sea. Frightened, the young woman runs off and Mathias heads back to town for lunch.

Since he still has not made good his announced visit to the Mareks, after lunch he goes to visit them. As he arrives, he realizes there is a heated argument going on and he quietly stands outside the kitchen listening to Robert Marek accusing his son, Julien, of having gone to the cliff the day before while Jacqueline was watching her sheep and perhaps even of having pushed her off the cliff in revenge for some harm she had done him earlier. Julien's defense is that at the time Jacqueline was probably killed, between 11:30 and 12:30 the day before, he was at home waiting outside the locked house for Robert to come home. This is the same time that Mathias had claimed to have gone to see the Mareks when he met Mme Marek on the road. When the Mareks notice that Mathias is there, and naturally assuming that Mathias had told Mme Marek the truth about his visit to the farm, Robert asks him whether he can corroborate Julien's story, whether he had seen Julien when he was at the farm the day before. Realizing that his story to Mme Marek conflicts with Julien's, Mathias uneasily admits that he did not see Julien. To Mathias's surprise, however, instead of insisting that Mathias never appeared at the farm house, Julien supports Mathias's alibi. Mathias leaves, puzzled and troubled at the fact that Julien lied to support Mathias's alibi. Rather than returning to town, Mathias goes back once again to the cliff and as he looks over the edge he sees Jacqueline's sweater hanging on the edge of a rock jutting out of the cliff wall. He immediately climbs down the dangerous side of the cliff to where the sweater is caught and tosses it into the sea. As he prepares to climb back up, he sees that Julien has been watching him. Julien tells him that he knows that that was Jacqueline's sweater, that he knows that Mathias did not go to the Marek farm the day before, and that he himself had found a cigarette butt, a piece of rope, and a candy wrapper in the grass on the cliff; then Julien disappears. Upset by all these events and suffering from a headache, Mathias makes his way back to the Café des Roches noires, where all the customers are discussing Jacqueline's death. He faints.

The next morning Mathias uses a cigarette to burn up a newspaper article he has been carrying around in his wallet which reports the death of another young woman. On his way to the café for breakfast he drops what is left of the bag of candy into a crevice. The café owner informs him that he has found a fisherman who would be willing to take Mathias back to the mainland if he were willing to leave right away. But Mathias refuses, giving feeble excuses for wanting to stay the extra day and wait for the regular ferry. His mind wanders to an image of Jacqueline tied down to the ground, hands behind her back, legs held apart, mouth stuffed with her blouse. Finally the next day Mathias catches the afternoon ferry back to the mainland.

Mathias's Guilt

The central event or nonevent in the book is the death of Jacqueline; however, the circumstances surrounding her death have constituted the major disagreement among critics discussing the book. Did Mathias go to the cliffs and rape, torture, and finally kill Jacqueline or not? Both the first part of the book

before her death and the second and third parts after her death
are oriented with reference to that blank space. The entire first
section is a preparation for the possibility of the murder of Jacqueline; the entire second part is a rewriting, a reinterpretation
of the facts and events aimed at removing the guilty aura from
them and allowing them to return to an uncharged, indifferent
status. In the second part of the book Mathias tries to untie the
links that had been created among objects and events and to retie
them in an innocent fashion. Robbe-Grillet gives the reader all
the reasons and proofs he needs to believe that Mathias is the
murderer. But he also gives the reader a blank page instead of
a crime and a series of scenes that could be the description of
Mathias's memories but could also be merely imagined; Mathias's
guilt can never be fixed. Robbe-Grillet is exploring instead the
way that the reader processes information given in the text and
tries to organize it into a logical pattern which will have a logical
and acceptable conclusion (acceptable, not in a moral sense but
in an artistic sense, i.e., in a sense that conforms to what the
reader has learned to expect in fiction). *Le Voyeur* contains all the
pieces for two puzzles, one in which Mathias is guilty and one
in which Mathias is innocent; but the last piece, the narrative
blank, fits neither puzzle alone and instead serves as a joint to
connect the two contradictory stories in the same way as the
figure X which appears on a movie poster in the port village ties
up the double circuit Mathias takes around the island, the two
lobes of the constantly recurring figure 8.

The narrative blank itself is echoed throughout the text in a
number of references to other missing details. In Mathias's youth-
ful drawing of a seagull, as perfect as it was, something seemed
to be missing; in the newspaper article's description of the murder
of a young girl, details of the murder were missing; even in the
description of the arrangement of glasses under the counter at the
bar, one glass is missing in the pattern. Nevertheless it is sometimes the recognition of the fact that a piece is missing that
allows the reconstruction of the whole pattern.

Robbe-Grillet builds up from the beginning the evidence
against Mathias, the pieces leading up to the recognition of a

pattern, not by describing Mathias as abnormal, but instead by dropping hints to the reader—the word violence here and there in innocent contexts, the waves of the sea slapping against each other, for example—that set up an anticipation in the reader of violence, of murder. Once this anticipation is established, the reader looks for the violent crime and interprets actions in the context of violence. The stage is set and the potential criminal and victim appear. In Part 1 when Mathias picks up the piece of cord while still on board the boat, the very next image he registers is that of the young girl seeming to stare at him. Her posture is suggestive of a person tied to a post, feet apart, hands behind her back. The cord, a potential accoutrement of torture wrapped into a figure 8, is now syntagmatically linked to the little girl. In a more explicit suggestion of violence, on board the ferry Mathias thinks over an ambiguous scene he had been witness to on his way to the dock that morning. As he walked down the street, he heard a muffled cry and through a nearby window this voyeur could see into a bedroom; over the disheveled bed stood a man holding his arm in the air looking at the bed. Like the other scenes suggestive of sex and violence in the book, there is no action in this scene, but the poses are sufficiently suggestive for both the reader and Mathias to complete the scene for themselves. Thus, by the time he arrives on the island, Mathias's mind (and the reader's mind) has already registered the suggestion of sex and violence, an object which might help carry out some perverted act, and a potential victim.

With this arrangement in place, and with an aura of suspicion created around such otherwise innocent acts as the purchase of a package of cigarettes and a bag of candy, and after the identification of a potential outlet for Mathias's building tension in Mme Leduc's wild young daughter Jacqueline, alone on the cliffs, a blank occurs in the work. Directly after this hole in the narrative, Mathias is shown to be anxious to establish where he was and what he was doing during the hour between the time that he rented the bicycle and the time that he ran into Mme Marek on the road near the place where the path leads off toward Jacqueline's cliff. The circumstantial evidence is against him.

Yet despite all the suggestions, all the evidence indicating that Mathias raped, tortured, and murdered the girl, there is still room for doubt. The murder itself is never described, only suggested. The objects involved in the torture take on an evil aura only if they are seen as objects of torture; after all a cord in itself is an innocent object, as are cigarettes, or candy, or the figure 8. The lapse of an hour or so in Mathias's timetable can be accounted for in various ways—he spent more time than he thought with Mme Leduc, he is subject to lapses of consciousness, he was mistaken about the time that he actually ran into Mme Marek. It is possible that Mathias's concern about finding alibis for himself, about retrieving half-smoked cigarettes reflects his fear that someone might misinterpret his innocent acts, that because he is a stranger on the island this evidence, however circumstantial, may tend to incriminate him. On the other hand Mathias may himself be fabricating a crime where none exists. His imagination is constantly at work plotting, figuring out, recreating scenes. If the long detailed descriptions in the book are taken to be seen through the protagonist's eyes, it is clear that his capacity for perception and his interest in registering minute details indicate an active mental life which he projects into the reality surrounding him. The suggestive elements around him on that day perhaps caused him to imagine himself killing Jacqueline. The most directly incriminating scene in the book is his confrontation with Julien Marek on the cliff, but the scene ends so abruptly that there is room to wonder whether the scene actually took place or whether Mathias had merely frightened himself into imagining the encounter.

In fact, however, Mathias's guilt and his innocence exist simultaneously. In *Le Voyeur* Robbe-Grillet constructs a fiction in which the possibility of such a murder is generated from the descriptions of ordinary objects which become invested with a potential for murder, torture, or rape. Mathias seems guilty because the objects he touches become charged. Yet this narrative is continuously superseded by a reconstruction being prepared at the same time using the same elements and postulating an erasure of the very connections that the first part had created. When

Mathias throws away the cigarette butts and the bag of candy, when he burns the newspaper clipping, all evidence connecting him to the crime is destroyed and therefore, the crime itself disappears. If these elements are eliminated from the work of fiction there can be no crime; there is nothing but the text, a construction of links between disparate signs where no links exist beforehand. In *Les Gommes* the use of the Oedipus myth created pretexual links among objects, links external to the text; in *Le Voyeur* the links are created with the text, not before it, by the juxtaposition of objects, by their double purposes, and by the ambiguous or suggestive terms used to describe them.

Parallel Oppositions

At the beginning of the book before Mathias's ferry has landed there is a description of an empty cigarette pack that someone on the pier had thrown into the water. At this point the pack of cigarettes is neutral; it is meant neither to embody any statement in reference to society or culture nor to carry symbolic weight nor to hide meaning behind its form. The object brings no meaning with it to the text; rather it takes on layers of significances as it becomes attached to other objects within the confines of the text. Thus, this pack of cigarettes serves as a joint that will allow the narrative to slip from one scene to any other in which an ordinary blue pack of cigarettes plays some role. In this instance at the very beginning, cigarettes become syntagmatically linked with erotic violence since this same type of ordinary cigarette appeared under the light on the table in the motionless suggestive scene Mathias had witnessed early that morning. When Mathias later buys such a pack of cigarettes, however innocent the purchase may be in itself, this first scene is being referred to and the suggestion of sexuality and violence is transferred to the pack of cigarettes he buys and becomes as much a basic characteristic of that pack as its blue color. The simple purchase of a pack of cigarettes is charged, not by connotations external to the text, but by the text itself.

When the pack hits the water, it bobs up and down with the waves: "Evenly and rhythmically, despite slight variations in

amplitude and rhythm . . . the sea rose and fell. . . . From
time to time at no doubt regular though complicated intervals,
a stronger movement would disrupt the rocking: two liquid
masses, coming towards each other, would hit with the sound
of a slap and a few drops of foam would splash a bit higher on
the wall" (15). The rhythm of the waves, their superficial and
their more profound, hidden periodicity, not always recognizable
as regular, the slapping sound that signals the predictable but
nevertheless surprising meeting of two different rhythms, and
the drops of foam like an ejaculation, which later reappear precisely in a scene in which Mathias allows his imagination to
explore and connect freely the violent and erotic actions that have
been suggested to him from the beginning of the book, these
three elements, the rhythm, the slap, and the foam associated
with the waves, lead to an essential movement in the text, engulfment. The empty pack of cigarettes is thrown into the waves,
for a time merely bobs up and down, and then is finally submerged
by the periodic clash of two waves. At the diegetic level, that
is, at the level of the arrangement of the elements of the plot,
the slapping sound and the drops of foam appear once again later
in the text and together with the disappearance of the cigarette
pack in the waves suggest one reading: in a context of violence
(slap), an ejaculation occurs (foam), and someone is eliminated,
killed. But there is no such act around which the book is structured; there is merely a hole, an engulfment, like a whirlpool,
sucking objects, characters, events into it. Like the pack of cigarettes submerged by the clap of two waves meeting, the crime,
the rape, torture, and murder of Jacqueline, is submerged, sucked
into a blank space by the movements of two contradictory im-
pulsions, one from one direction tending to realize, generate this
act, another from the opposite direction tending to erase, deny,
disintegrate it. The reality of the act, whether or not Mathias
committed the crime, cannot be determined since there is only
absence, negation of two opposite periodicities at that point.

These two opposite waves reflect another opposition exploited
throughout the novel at various levels. The two poles are the
source of a whole series of elements present in the book: on the

one hand, Mathias, water, darkness, regularity, predictability, social acceptance, repression; and on the other hand, Jacqueline, fire, light, spontaneity, unpredictability, social rejection, action. The opposition between these two conflicting series and the extension of each in its own direction helps account for certain events in the text. Mathias arrives on the island by water, and at several points in the text when events upset him, a view of the sea, the idea of its regular cadence, of its reach at once distant yet limited by the horizon, of its muted, unchanging aspect is calming and reassuring. Its power to stabilize and level emotions doubles when the water of the sea finds its duplicate in rain, in cloudy, cool weather, the kind of weather Mathias imagines when he remembers his childhood. "The weather was very calm, without a trace of wind. A light, fine, continuous rain fell, without violence, which, although it covered the horizon, was not enough to obscure the view at shorter distances. On the contrary, in this cleaned air the nearest objects benefited from an extra glow" (19). One scene in particular from his childhood comes back to him. The house behind him is dark; he is alone, quietly doing the portrait of a seagull he sees before him outside. The peace Mathias felt seated there all alone was augmented by his satisfaction at being praised for his perfect reproduction of the gull.

Days of light, dreary, calm rain are associated with a success that required patience, exactitude, detail. As an adult the same search for satisfaction and comfort in exactitude and detail emerges in Mathias's calculations of his potential watch sales, profits, time spent per sale, time spent per nonsale. Furthermore, when confronted with an emotional situation or one in which he perceives imminent danger, Mathias seeks refuge in these exact details; he operates a shift in the level of his perception of reality and hides or controls his emotion by focusing on the safe aspects of the world around him, on its exact physical characteristics. During his visit to the Marek farm, as he listens to the accusations made against Julien, accusations, as he realizes, very threatening to himself and his alibis, Mathias focuses on the safe aspects of the scene, not on the dangerous voices and words, but on the indifferent, unthreatening, unaccusing props surrounding the people. "In the gap, ten or fifteen centimeters wide, only a corner of the table was visible, where, on the oilcloth covered with little multicolored flowers, there lay a pair of glasses, a carving knife, and two unequal piles of white dishes—clean—placed side by side" (192–93). The field of vision is restricted to that permitted by a narrow opening in the wall separating Mathias from his potential accusers, an opening narrow enough so that the amount he perceives is limited, controllable. Moreover, when Mathias is confronted by Julien on the cliff, he is so upset he actually begins to recite multiplication tables (216); a fixed, orderly series that Mathias has learned and will make no mistakes on, the multiplication tables are ideal to allow Mathias's mind to regain control of itself, protect itself, repress awareness of danger.

Although he seeks comfort in these details, Mathias is also aware that this taste for precision verges on obsession. "Such concern for precision—unusual, excessive, suspect—far from making him seem innnocent, wasn't it actually incriminating?" (227). This same excessive precision, far from giving an impression of accurately reproduced reality, like the portrait of the sea gull, instead suggests the quality of perception associated with hallucination and thereby adds to the ambiguity of the book; how many levels of reality are involved in the descriptions of Mathias's perceptions? The reference points available to the reader are increasingly undermined as the narrative progresses.

Mathias, too, looks for points of reference in his attempts to process reality. In order to gauge, for example, the progress of the ferry toward the dock, Mathias picks out the 8 form etched into the rock near the landing. His search for reference points extends to all his movements, actions, relationships. Lacking an innate sense of the appropriate response to situations, Mathias, like Wallas before him in *Les Gommes*, has had to memorize specific responses to specific stimuli, sales pitches in a sense. In several scenes, for example, Mathias practices, actually or simply mentally, opening his sample case, moving the appointment book, removing the protective covering, and displaying a group of watches. These actions are safe; Mathias knows how to perform them perfectly if only given a chance. Confronted with a situation for which he has not rehearsed, however, or with people who refuse to play by the rules of social convention Mathias has assimilated, he has difficulty containing his confusion and frustration. His old friend Pierre or Jean Robin and his wife (or his servant or his daughter) frustrate Mathias in just this way; she says nothing and his outbursts are incomprehensible: "Here again Mathias found him in a situation where it was impossible to act according to any rule whatever, which he could have referred to later—which could have directed his behavior—behind which he could have, if necessary, hidden" (144).

Mathias is never absolutely sure what to say, how to say it, how to react; but he tries desperately to absorb lessons on correct behavior from those around him. Mathias cannot invent verbal responses; he can only remember them: ". . . he could not remember what it was appropriate to say in this particular situation" (71). "The traveler wondered if he ought to reply" (137). The man who runs the tobacco store and garage gives Mathias a lesson in stimulus/response. Commenting on a woman who walks by, he says, "Nice looking girl! Huh? (47)." "As a professional courtesy" (48), Mathias winks in agreement. But he soon realizes he has made a mistake; the man's comments had been a trap and like all words represent danger for Mathias. Mathias's answer is wrong. "Oh sure! As far as pretty girls are concerned. . . . You could just eat them up" (51). "—Well, you sure are easy to please! They are all horrible in this land of alcoholics" (51).

Words are dangerous because they can indicate an incorrect attitude and reveal too much. On the other hand silence is equally unacceptable. Mathias imagines an entire scenario of himself selling watches to the Leducs in complete silence: ". . . the entire scene remained ridiculously silent. . . . He could see he would have to start all over again" (36). Like the voice in Beckett's *L'Innommable,* he is forced to talk, but what he says is always wrong. Words are slippery; they have too many meanings. Mathias may intend one thing, and his interlocutor may understand something different, something which may incriminate Mathias. Thus, he must plan his words carefully.

The concern with planning ahead emerges in many of Mathias's actions, and Mathias finds any disruption of his plans annoying, at the least. He had not planned on having to wait for a bicycle; he had not planned on beginning his sales in town; he views these changes in his plans as bad omens. Even when his plans are impossible to realize, Mathias insists on following them. He reproaches himself not for failing to sell many watches but for the unsystematic way he has been carrying on his sales despite the carefully calculated, totally unachievable plans he had devised before his arrival.

Mathias's attempts at precision, at preplanning, and at propriety are all attempts to organize, and therefore to control, the world around him. This same purpose motivates the many scenes in which Mathias makes résumés of his past or future actions. After descriptions of the sea gull he drew as a child, of the items in his briefcase, of his actions when selling watches, he repeats the descriptions in summary, picking up the major points again and making them clear and controllable. But as Mathias summarizes the text of his visit to Mme Leduc, the summary goes out of control: "The whole beginning took place very quickly: . . . the wristwatches . . . , the big kitchen, the table in the middle of the room, the oilcloth . . . , the pressure of fingers on the latch of the briefcase, the cover swinging open, the black appointment book, the pamphlets, the rectangular frame set on the buffet, the shiny metal brace, the photograph, the path heading down, the hollow on the cliff sheltered from the wind, secret, quiet, isolated as if by the thickest walls . . . as if by the thickest walls . . ." (117). With the mention of the photograph the description begins to veer off in a dangerous direction, mirroring the possibility that Mathias too veered off the main path after leaving Mme Leduc's. To protect Mathias, his summary must jump back again to a point where the description is still safe; the summary begins again and once again is blocked by the word "photograph": ". . . the shiny metal frame, the photograph which showed . . . the photograph which showed, the photograph, the photograph, the photograph, the photograph . . ." (117).

These résumés are attempts, successful or not, to arrange events and objects in a linear pattern which allows Mathias to deal with only one incident at a time. None of the events can have ramifications other than that of inserting the subsequent event into the straight line of events; each event is defined, like numbers in a series, strictly by its position before and after another event.[2] Furthermore, by making these résumés Mathias insists on the idea that only those events which he includes, only those that lead directly to the end he desires have any weight in the text. Those annoying events that refuse to line up in an orderly and innocent sequence are discounted and eliminated. In Mathias's world there is no room for tangents, for spontaneity. Everything must lead smoothly and in an orderly fashion to a predictable result. This orderly linear arrangement is what a traditional linear reading requires, but such a reading of a Robbe-Grillet text is doomed to failure because it insists upon the same kind of regular sequence, the kind Mathias attempts to maintain, from a work of fiction which refuses to conform to the idea that only directly causal relationships are real and can therefore appear in fiction. Like the word "photograph" there are insistent obstacles to this kind of linear reading which cannot be ignored.

Cautious, controlled, and conforming, when confronted with the emotional disruptions represented by suggestions of sexuality or violence, Mathias cannot deal with their unpredictability. His sensitivity to such disruptions strains his ability to function according to his plans. The most disruptive figure in the text is Mathias's counterpoint, Jacqueline, associated with fire, spontaneity, refusal to conform. At the beginning of the book as his boat approaches the island, Mathias notices a young girl who becomes syntagmatically associated with cigarettes, thus by extension fire and light. At this point in the novel the light of the morning sun is alternately described as very brilliant or slightly hazy, but neither oppressive to Mathias nor a sign of emotional turmoil.

Light quickly becomes associated with Jacqueline and with sexual violence, however. On his way to the port in the morning Mathias had been witness to the scene suggestive of sexual violence; in that silent scene despite the daylight outside, a lamp near the bed was lit, illuminating the ordinary blue package of cigarettes (fire). Later, on the island, Mathias enters another room empty and silent. A picture of a little girl saying her evening prayers hangs on the wall. Lamplight falls on her shoulder and neck and with the mention of the lamp, this scene is suddenly superimposed upon the earlier scene; the sadistic potential of that earlier scene is transferred to this new one by means of a conduit common to both scenes, the light of the lamp. The tension of sexual violence builds in the second room; the girl in the picture is on her knees, the bed in the room is in disorder, the bedcover, hanging half on the floor, is red, suggestive of both violence and sex, and finally, "A kind of heat was coming from the room, as though some fireplace were still lit, at this time of year" (68). Suddenly Mathias leaves, almost flees from the apartment to the outside, where he still feels overwarm, "his mind on other things" (69), things hinted at but not further specified here. By the time Mathias arrives at Mme Leduc's house, he is ready to transfer onto the picture of Jacqueline the tension built up by the confusion in his mind of the two scenes; he confuses Jacqueline's name and calls her Violette, sugesting both violence and rape (*viol* in French). Mme Leduc exacerbates the strain on Mathias as she complains that her daughter is uncontrollable, refuses to obey, to conform; "she has the devil in her . . ." (83). When she calls her daughter a witch, the final link is forged between Jacqueline and the fires of witch burnings. Mathias is all but charged with a mission: to eliminate the aberration and disorder Jacqueline embodies. As in the case of the witches to which her mother had compared her, the townspeople too found Jacqueline's failure to conform and her refusal to be controlled intolerable; they give their tacit approval to her elimination by never suspecting Mathias of the murder.

The Search for Congruency

On another level, however, Jacqueline/Violette is merely the name for the space in the text in which Mathias's schedule was the most out of kilter with itself. *Le Voyeur* is a study in the coordination of time and space, which are not congruent here, not placed evenly one on the other, and this imbalance, this messy irregularity like Jacqueline must be eliminated. The rectification takes four days, the days Mathias spends on the island. Once the adjustment in Mathias's schedule is made and all the repercussions of the original disharmony are played out, Mathias no longer needs to flee the island. *Le Voyeur* is the story of that readjustment of time to eliminate about an hour. The first mention of a small imperfection in the coordination of time and space occurs as the ferry reaches the island in the morning: " 'It's on time today,' one voice said. And someone corrected: 'Almost.' " (12). The time-space problem becomes the central issue; at what time did Mathias occupy what space? Before Mathias can devote himself entirely to this problem, he must complete the first cycle of his double loop trajectory around the island to sell his watches. Since his lost hour is still not accounted for by the end of that first cycle, his timing still not synchronized, he is unable to reach the return ferry on time; his shouts and gestures calling the boat back are misinterpreted as good-byes and he is left on the island.

But now he can devote full time to completing the second cycle of action, the one which began with the sight of an ambiguous bedroom scene and reached its peak with the blank space in the text. There are many possible ways to rewrite the text of the blank page, both texts that would exonerate and texts that would incriminate Mathias. Mathias is desperately trying to organize the elements of the text to prove himself innocent. On the cliff with Julien, at each of Mathias's attempts to construct a logical innocent sequence of events, Julian opens the possibility of other combinations of the same elements but combinations which implicate Mathias in Jacqueline's murder. In his frustration at seeing an innocent interpretation of his actions slipping away, Mathias takes the position of the writer of fiction: "He could have said just as easily that the gray wool sweater was not 'among the rocks,' but 'hanging on the edge of the rock'—or that only one of the mahonias was ready to bloom at his father's farm. . . . Or that the unaccounted for time at the Marek's intersection was not forty minutes. The traveler had not gotten to that part of his

circuit before ten or fifteen minutes before twelve noon . . ."
(218–19).

All the preciseness about time and place, all the corrections
that both Julien and Mathias try to make in Robbe-Grillet's text,
justified by the notion that Mathias either really killed Jacqueline
or did not, are irrelevant. There is no correct text; there is no
reality of which *Le Voyeur* is an account. The logic of fiction is
not the logic of reality, and therefore everything, even the identity
of the main character, can fluctuate. Thus, at one point at the
Café des Roches noires, Mathias begins to disintegrate as descriptions of events and objects in the fiction, truth and falsehood,
become superimposed upon each other. Mathias, the watch salesman, is suddenly described as talking to the watch salesman.
Like Dr. Jekyll and Mr. Hyde, he is split into the normal,
innocent salesman, the *voyageur,* and the guilty sadistic murderer,
the *voyeur.*[3]

By the end of this day Mathias has completed a second, innocent
trip around the southern loop of his double loop itinerary and
with the completion of this loop, the danger is over for Mathias
because all the incriminating events of the first trajectory exist
in at least one innocent version just as Mathias exists as the *voyeur*
and the *voyageur.* The next morning as Mathias awakens, the
change that has occurred is apparent. As though he had discovered
that he and his crime only exist as fiction, Mathias is able con-
fidently to destroy the few remaining fragments of evidence connecting him to the crime. He even refuses to take the opportunity
offered him by the café owner to return to the safety of the
mainland early because, he says, "I don't like to make decisions
at the last minute. . . . I'm not in that much a hurry" (243).
Time has caught up with itself and therefore no longer poses a
problem. As Mathias's ferry leaves, he watches a buoy bobbing
up and down in the water, just as an ordinary blue pack of
cigarettes had done at the beginning. His long curved nails,
which had made him uneasy at the beginning of the book, have
still not been cut short, but they no longer signify anything to
Mathias; they are no longer a threat, a sign of Mathias's guilt.
They have retreated back into the indifferent world of objects like

the buoy which merely exist, without being signs to interpret; their meanings have been erased. And the announcement made at the beginning of the novel comes true, "It was as if no one had heard" (9). Or as if no crime had been committed, no story had been written. The knitting together of the elements of the text has been unraveled. What had been encoded into the text, Robbe-Grillet has decoded and dissipated.

Chapter Four

La Jalousie

By 1957 when *La Jalousie* appeared Robbe-Grillet's reputation as an experimental novelist was already well established.[1] Since objects and geometrical descriptions were playing such a large part in his work and the role of human psychology and personal histories was not apparent, Robbe-Grillet was accused of presenting a cold, flat, mechanical universe from which man was banned and which was therefore, some felt, of no interest to man. At the same time Robbe-Grillet was destroying the traditional novel form, the form of humanistic literary expression par excellence. Robbe-Grillet's defense expressed in his critical essays which were appearing at this time in *L'Express* was to maintain that in fact in his works man was put squarely in the center of the universe, for how can objects be seen, described, or even exist if not for man's perception of them? All objects are seen through human eyes; if man were absent from Robbe-Grillet's universe, there would be no universe.

As if to illustrate more clearly this position, in *La Jalousie* the entire novel moves through the consciousness of a single man who never himself appears or is described, just as one is never present to one's own consciousness, but rather one's own existence is postulated based on one's capacity to register perceptions. Robbe-Grillet himself suggested the organizing factor in the novel: a jealous husband who spies on his wife, A..., and is suspicious of her relationship with a neighbor, Franck. The sensations and perceptions of this husband, which constitute the novel, are filtered through a mind distorted by jealousy. These distortions find their echo in a defective window pane which distorts images seen through it and in the window shades (*les jalousies,* the same word in French as for jealousy) or venetian blinds through which the husband spies on his wife's activities and which also distort anything perceived through them by limiting the optical range to the openings between the slats.

The novel is not organized chronologically; that is, no accurate chronological sequence of events can be established because of the many repetitions of scenes often with ambiguous variations. The narrator's perhaps pathological distortions of his descriptions of the sights, sounds, and events surrounding him disrupt the narrative's chronology in the same way as Mathias's memories and fantasies did in *Le Voyeur*. Furthermore, because the book is written primarily in the present tense, several critics have disagreed with Bruce Morrissette's description of the movement of this narrative as duplicating the life of an emotion, jealousy, tracing its beginning, its paroxysm during A...'s absence, and its appeasement upon her return. Rather than this linear development other critics have seen a circular development with all the events bound to repeat themselves. "In *La Jalousie*, we have a perfectly circular structure, in which the present indicative attests to the immobility of time. This explains why the order of the scenes in the book is of no chronological importance since it is condemned to repetition."[2]

Nevertheless, events of the novel can be summarized even if their exact order cannot be given. The book is divided into nine sections; a good number of the elements which will go into the construction of the novel are presented in the first section through the vision, here and throughout, of the first person narrator, who is never described and seems to take no part in the action but to whom the others in the novel nevertheless do respond. The book opens with a long precise description of the shadow made by a post at the southwest corner of a house supporting a roof over a terrace. The house is on a banana plantation somewhere, probably in the West Indies, or perhaps Africa. A woman who is only referred to as A..., apparently the wife of the narrator, is described standing in her room, then brushing her hair, then reading or writing a letter. In later descriptions this letter seems to turn up in the pocket of Franck, the owner of the neighboring plantation. A scene is described at a dinner with the narrator,

A..., and Franck, who has arrived, as the narrator says, once again without his wife Christiane, who has remained at home with their young son. From the manner in which Franck and A... are described, the narrator gives the impression that they have a rather special relationship to each other which excludes him. His descriptions of their conversations about Franck's troubles with his truck and about a novel which Franck has lent A... and which is set in a situation similar to that of *La Jalousie* itself are interspersed with descriptions of the dining room in which they are eating and the terrace on which they have before-dinner drinks and after-dinner coffee.

This first section then serves as an introduction to the setting, the characters, and the conflicts among them. The rest of the book combines, adds to, and analyzes the elements set forth. It becomes increasingly clear that the narrator spies on A..., often through the venetian blinds covering the window of her bedroom, and suspects her of having a romantic interest in Franck. The narrator's only other major interest seems to be his house and his plantation which he describes at great length, mentioning exactly how many plots of banana trees he has planted in how many rows of how many banana trees per row. But despite all this exactness, the narrator makes inexplicable changes in his descriptions of the same plots of trees or in his descriptions of his house. These variations suggest that the action and the descriptions take place over a certain period of time as the banana trees grow, are cut down, and are replanted. Yet the narrator recounts everything in the present tense and often begins his descriptions with the time indicator "now," even when the event or the state described must be a part of the past and not a scene he is seeing as he speaks. Thus, the chronology of the novel becomes too intricate to be disentangled. The cause of these variations has been attributed to the distortions caused by a jealousy that has gone beyond the limits of sanity.

There are two basic events in the novel to which the narrator continuously returns and which serve to orient the reader in his attempt to follow the development. First at some point during the dinner with Franck, A..., and the narrator (or during one of the dinners since it is not clear if there is only one or several), A... sees a centipede on a wall in the dining room. Realizing that she is upset by the sight of this creature, Franck rolls up his napkin, crushes the centipede against the wall, and finishes it off by stepping on it after it falls to the floor. This simple sequence is described seven times; in one case instead of being its normal size, a few inches long, the centipede grows to the size of a dinner plate with enormous legs, antennae, and mouth parts, which make a grating sound as the insect dies. The scene of the killing of the centipede is obviously disturbing to the narrator, who returns to it so often that it finally becomes a reminder of the whole relationship the narrator suspects between A... and Franck and a signal of the narrator's distress at it.

Preparation for the second scene begins immediately after the centipede scene. Franck has had some trouble with his truck and in order to repair it he will be forced to drive to the port town some four hours away. Learning of the possibility of getting a ride into town, A... decides she will accompany Franck. On the day of A...'s trip into town with Franck, the narrator's activities are not described in detail until night falls, after he has had dinner alone and the hour of A...'s expected return approaches. The narrator describes in minute detail everything he does that evening: he sits on the porch watching insects fly around a lamp, he walks through the house and notices the patterns on the floors and the construction of the walls, he tries to scrape off or erase the stain left on the wall where the centipede was crushed. As the time for A...'s return draws nearer, his anxiety seems to intensify and not only the stain on the dining room wall reappears but the centipede itself is there grown to enormous proportions. Suddenly the narrator begins to see scenes of A... and Franck in a hotel room together, in bed together, and finally in Franck's car as it swerves out of control, hits a tree, and bursts into flames.

The next morning A... and Franck have still not returned and a messenger sent by Christiane informs the narrator of her own concern. Finally around noon, in a scene already described earlier in the novel, A... and Franck return, blaming their delay on the fact that the car, a new car which had run perfectly up to that

point, broke down, forcing them to spend the night in town.
There is an odd exchange of comments between A... and Franck
regarding his lack of ability as a mechanic. The novel ends with
one of the already familiar scenes in the novel which depicts the
three characters on the terrace together, the narrator silent as A...
and Franck discuss again the African novel Franck has lent her.

Point of View

The most immediately noticeable difference in the disposition
of this novel from that of traditional novels is Robbe-Grillet's
manipulation of the point of view. Having long before rejected
the technique of employing an omniscient author,[3] in *La Jalousie*
Robbe-Grillet went a step further and challenged narration in
first person as well. The narrative obviously emerges from the
kind of single specific vantage point usually localized in a particular character normally designated by he, she, or I; however,
no such pronoun is used to refer to the narrative voice. Names
are not interchangeable as they are in *Le Voyeur;* Franck and
Christiane designate two specific characters whose attributes remain centered upon them as their names do. Although designated
only by a letter, A... too has stable, recognizable features. The
real problem is who is speaking. When the novel first appeared,
Robbe-Grillet made the statement, which he later regretted, that
the narrator is A...'s excessively jealous husband. Since then,
although there is no real textual evidence to support this idea
directly, critics and readers have taken Robbe-Grillet's remark
as the key to *La Jalousie* and have referred to this narrator as
A...'s husband. The narrator does not refer to himself as "I," this
"I" being altogether coextensive with the thinking itself. One
critic who has objected to the position that there is a husband
who relates the events of the novel is Maurice Blanchot: "[the
reader] clearly senses that something is missing, he has the feeling
that it is this absence which allows everything to be said and to
be seen, but how can this absence be identified with anyone?
How could there actually be a name there and an identity? It is
without a name, without a face; it is pure anonymous presence."[4]
This is certainly the only conclusion justified by the text; never-

theless, the reader confronted with this "pure anonymous presence," through which the novel exists and on which each description and event in the text depends, inevitably postulates not only a character through whose eyes he can see but also a personality for the character which allows the reader to justify the organization of the perceptions registered. Why do certain events and descriptions recur, often in distorted forms? Why does this "anonymous presence" insistently seem to spy on the actions of A...? The suggestion that this spy is A...'s husband seems reasonable.

Having thus constituted the narrative center of *La Jalousie,* by logical extension, critics and readers made pathological jealousy the main point of reference necessary for the understanding of the novel and capable of accounting for all aspects of the text. Only one other important approach to the interpretation of the novel has been formulated, the brilliant sociologically based study by Jacques Leenhardt, which argues with great coherence that the novel's center is not a husband's jealousy but his fear, as an old-style colonialist in Africa, of being dispossessed of his wife and his property.[5]

Fear of Dispossession

The action of *La Jalousie* is extremely localized. Whereas in both *Les Gommes* and *Le Voyeur* the peregrinations of the central character played a major role not only in the action of the novel but in its very structure, in *La Jalousie* movement is almost limited to the changing focus of the eyes of the husband. Although the husband seems to move around the house and the terrace, he never leaves his refuge and is satisfied to limit his range of perceptions to what may be discerned from this central point. As a result, these descriptions of this limited area in Robbe-Grillet's short, bare sentences produce a feeling of confinement. Furthermore, the house is not a perfect refuge. The sounds of the wild forest infiltrate the house at night; insects like the centipede can penetrate even into the dining room. The greatest threat to the husband's tranquility, Franck, not only has the right to invade the house but even more upsetting threatens to dispossess this owner of his property by removing A... from her prison home.

The narrator's fear of dispossession produces the organizing principle of the text, which is the idea of seeing as a means of possession or control.[6] The fact that the narrator oversees the natives' work on his plantation but never participates in it establishes his rank as privileged; they work for him and therefore he controls them. But his need to control the potentially unruly natives extends beyond merely their work. The natives, the workers, belong to life outside the house, outside civilization. Like the banana trees planted in neat rows which they tend, they have been organized, but the potential for reverting to a natural state is implied in the juxtaposition of the planted banana trees to the south of the house with the forest which has overrun the crops and repossessed the territory to the north of the house. Putting the banana trees into neat rows, making tallies of their number, describing in detail, not their appearance, not the form of the leaves or the rough spots on the trunks, but their positions are all indications of the narrator's attempts to organize unruly reality, to impose on it a structure. The source of his power to control comes from his ability to see.[7]

By the same token the narrator's spying on A... is his attempt to control her. As long as he can watch her, she remains his possession. If she gets out of his range of vision, he alleviates the resulting anxiety by fixing his sight on something he can control. Thus when his chair is placed in such a way that he cannot see A... and Franck behind him, he tries to describe the scene before him. Unfortunately for him it is dark, and night is the enemy of sight. But as he touches the banister surrounding the porch, protecting him from the night, which belongs to the natives, to the insects, and to nature, the reminder of this friendly barrier against the uncontrollable operates a switch from the uncomfortable scene in which he cannot see to a detailed description of the banister.

The venetian blinds play an important role in the quest for control of A.... Robbe-Grillet describes these blinds: "A *jalousie* is a kind of window shutter which allows a person to see out through it and at certain angles to see in through it; but when the blinds are closed you cannot see anything, in either direction."[8] Thus, the narrator can watch A... without her being aware of his gaze. Beyond their diegetic function, however, these blinds also help the narrator organize reality. Instead of being confronted with the whole mass of reality outside his house all at once, when he looks through the blinds the narrator finds this reality carefully and evenly divided into manageable portions. The sections actually blocked out do not disturb him. In fact on one occasion the narrator's view is cut first into horizontal spaces by the blinds and then again vertically by the posts holding up the banister: ". . . there remains only a series of little squares representing a very small part of the total surface—perhaps a ninth" (32). With eight-ninths of his vision cut off, he may not see much of the surface of his garden through the grill of the blinds and the posts but he feels he can be sure of what he sees.

His desire to break up the world into manageable pieces extends to a tendency to fragment people, referring to Franck, for example, as the shirt, to a native as the brown arm, to A... as the mass of dark hair, and finally, in a rare reference to himself as the eye. This fragmentation is an inevitable by-product of description, for no object can be described in words other than one feature at a time, indeed one word at a time, and the fragmentation increases in proportion to the detail of the description. Thus, the narrator's tendency to fragment meets the requirements of both the narrative and the narrator. Although fragmentation inevitably produces holes, missing parts, incompletion, these gaps do not disturb the narrator. Looking through the blinds, the narrator misses eight-ninths of the scene. The narrator himself is missing from the narrative. During one dinner from which Franck is absent, his absence is not described simply as absence but as the presence of a hole, the presence of something missing, a blank space between the edge of the table and the back of the chair. The narrator also notes the missing parts of his plantation: in such and such a row of banana trees there should be twenty-three trees, not only twenty-two; but neither absence nor fragmentation is upsetting so long as the narrator can name, count, or describe the missing pieces.

Leenhardt explores the counterpoint to this limited, but organized view of the world by comparing the static, linear separation of reality by the blinds into manageable and undistorted spaces to the distortions created in the narrator's vision when he looks to the north through a window. A circular imperfection in the window glass causes the scene to float disturbingly. Seen through the circular distortion, parts of the uncultivated banana tree plot north of the house seem to be growing up in the form of circles or crescents in the yard or on the truck parked there. The uncultivated northern section of the plantation threatens to move into the yard surrounding the house, to end order and civilization.[9]

Panic at the idea of being thus dispossessed of his territory, his life style, and his wife causes the narrator to produce his own distortions as he walks around his house during A...'s trip to town with Franck. A...'s being out of his sight means her being out of his control as well. Up to this point the narrator's descriptions of A... had been descriptions of her appearance and actions while she was within range of his sight. Although obviously disturbed by some of the behavior he observed, the narrator never specifically speculated on the possibility of a clandestine romance between A... and Franck. Once they are no longer controlled by his gaze, however, the narrator openly presumes the sexual nature of their relationship. The repeated description of the centipede's death, associated with the possibility of a relationship between Franck and A..., produces scenes which have perhaps really been in the narrator's mind all along but which he has been trying to deny by describing indifferent objects. The scene in which a trip to town is first mentioned is followed immediately by the first detailed description of A...'s sighting of the centipede and Franck's killing it. Thus, the trip to town and the centipede are syntagmatically linked.

But in his review of the events surrounding the killing of the centipede the narrator's memory of the events and his fabrication of new events overlap: "Franck, without saying a word, stands up, wads his napkin into a ball. . . . Then, with his foot, he squashes it [the centipede] against the bedroom floor" (112). The word bedroom distorts the time, place, and meaning of Franck's action since the centipede scene had always taken place in the dining room before and not in a bedroom. The sexual implications only latent in the previous descriptions of the act of killing the centipede are actualized: "Then he comes back toward the bed and in passing hangs the towel on its metal rack near the wash-bowl" (112). In the context of this relationship between A... and Franck which the narrator has opened to his imagination, A...'s previous actions are reviewed and become sexually charged. "The hand with the tapering fingers has clenched into a fist on the white sheet" (113). A...'s hand grasps what in other descriptions had been a table knife, then a tablecloth, then an ambiguous cloth, and finally becomes a bedsheet. Furthermore, the narrator combines the description of the lovemaking he imagines between A... and Franck with the description of their deaths, superimposing the two sequels by means of descriptions common to both scenes. A... is on the bed; Franck walks toward her. Her hand grips the bedsheet in a paroxysm; the mosquito netting falls. "In his haste to reach his goal, Franck increases his speed. The jolts become more violent" (113). Up to this point these actions are still in the context of the bedroom and seem to indicate lovemaking. But the next sentence wrenches away the intolerable bedroom scene and replaces it with a realization of the narrator's desire to punish the transgressors. "In the darkness he has not seen the hole running halfway across the road. The car makes a leap, skids. . . . On this bad road the driver cannot straighten out in time. The blue sedan is going to crash into a roadside tree whose rigid foliage scarcely shivers under the impact, despite its violence. The car immediately bursts into flames. The whole brush is illuminated by the crackling, spreading fire. It is the sound the centipede makes, motionless again on the wall, in the center of the panel" (113). The description thus comes full circle, back to the centipede scene which had set it off. The potential loss of A... latent in all the narrator's descriptions of her but always safely controlled is realized once she escapes from his controlling sight.

Invasion

Equally disturbing as this fantasied loss of A... is the invasion of the narrator's once safe and protective house. As night falls, the threatening darkness robs the narrator of his ability to see. As soon as the light, representative of civilization, is gone, noises from the wilds surrounding the house arise and penetrate the house. No natural sound is innocent; even A...'s brushing her hair recalls to the mind of the narrator the remembered or imagined crackling sound the centipede made when it was crushed. This sound is then repeated in the fire which the narrator imagines engulfs A... and Franck after the car accident on the night of A...'s absence. The narrator manages to protect himself for a time with an artificial light from the gas lamp (a lamp that A . . . has objected to using, preferring darkness on the terrace) which not only provides light but makes noise as well, this noise constituting a reminder of civilization and not a dangerous natural noise: "But the lamp prevents any such sound from being heard because of its constant hissing, of which the ear is aware only when it tries to hear any other sound" (99). But on this night the protection is not completely effective: "Shrill and short, an animal's cry sounds quite close, seeming to come from the garden, just at the foot of the veranda. Then the same cry, after three seconds, indicates its presence on the other side of the house. And again there is silence, which is not silence but a succession of identical, shriller, more remote cries in the mass of the banana trees near the stream, perhaps on the opposite slope, reaching from one end of the valley to the other" (101). An army of thousands, the unknown creatures creating these noises surround the house and even seem to signal their positions to each other. They come from the "mass of the banana trees" no longer in neat rows, controlled by a civilizing gaze, but reverted back to an unorganized mass, unorganized and therefore dangerous.

Even the light from the lamp is problematic. It attracts the invasive insects to it and they fly in patterns the narrator tries to follow, a confusing series: "loops, garlands, sudden ascents and brutal falls, changes of direction, abrupt retracings . . ." (103), not meaningful or regular, controlled, and reassuring. The gas lamp also alters the nature of the house itself. Certain elements of the house are less distinct; certain dimensions are exaggerated; but worst the house begins to sway: "The slight swaying of the lamp advancing along the hallway animates the uninterrupted series of chevrons with a continual undulation like that of waves" (110). Thus, the house itself seems to be slipping out of the narrator's control.

In this atmosphere of tense anxiety the image made by the centipede on the wall is exaggerated to its most menacing proportions. The seven recurrences of the centipede scene indicate its importance in this book. Gradually, the centipede takes on meaning as the converging point, the objective support, for the narrator's inadequacies, his jealousy, and his dispossession. The enormous centipede the narrator sees on the wall during A...'s absence is bloated with all the connotations that have been attached to it in each previous appearance; the text gives the centipede its significance.

A...

Although on the whole she fits quite well into the narrator's dream of a *permanence d'ensemble* ("general stability"), A... poses a threat to the narrator. As Leenhardt points out, like Franck, she is certainly a part of the world of the white colonialist. But she is a woman and is therefore necessarily, like the native population, subjugated and made into an object by the same processes that give the narrator his dominance over the native population. Like the narrator's servants and workers, she exists at the outer edge of the narrator's control. Her room seems to be a prison cell formed by the horizontal bars of the venetian blinds at all three windows and by the walls of the room made of a kind of paneling forming vertical bars. The narrator, aware of his somewhat tenuous control over this creature, at once like him and different from him, twice imagines her escape; just as she can escape his gaze by moving into certain corners of the bedroom, she is capable of simply walking out the door, through the hall, and out of the house toward the uncontrolled, uncultivated fields of banana trees where the narrator has no power.

Like many of the female figures in Robbe-Grillet's later works, A... has a certain capacity for fluidity, an inherent freedom, which to a small extent she shares here with Franck by comparison with the rigidity of the narrator. She clearly escapes Franck as well, however, putting herself on the other side of the line between masters and slaves, on the side which allows her to pass judgments on her keepers. The judgments are sexual. While any sexual link between A... and the narrator is simply not mentioned, the unavoidably sexual tone of his descriptions of her brushing her hair indicates a desire on his part that is never resolved. There is no evidence that he and A... occupy the same bedroom, this suggested separation perhaps indicating a sexual impotency in the narrator/husband which emerges at other levels as a failure to act at all, even in his own interests. The success of the sexual link postulated by the narrator between A... and Franck seems doubtful, however. In the scene which takes place after the return of A... and Franck from town, the conversation about Franck's not being a very good mechanic, Franck's apologies to A... for not having been able to do a better job of making her comfortable, and Franck's expression, a kind of grin from which the humor drains while the grimace remains, all seem to indicate that A... is no more in Franck's camp than in that of the narrator. While Franck is incredulous at the idea of the European woman in the African novel regarding a black native as sexually desirable, A... finds nothing unreasonable about such a desire.

A...'s double affiliation, with the masters and with the slaves, is revealed in her manner of being. Although A... is always correct in her eating habits, well balanced standing or sitting, restrained in her speech, and self-assured, the narrator emphasizes what he feels is her natural and therefore incomprehensible grace, epitomized in her long hair. Her hair, on which the narrator centers his sexual desire, poses no problem to him as long as she is in her prison-cell bedroom brushing it, as the narrator says, mechanically, that is, in a manner in harmony with her role as one of the masters. When she leaves that sanctuary, however, the repository of the narrator's confidence in ownership, she puts her hair up into a coiffure which the narrator describes as chaotic and unstable, and therefore dangerous. Her hair materializes the narrator's feeling of ownership and at the same time his fears of losing his control over A.... A... exists somewhere between the world of civilization and the chaotic world of the natives.

When it first appeared, *La Jalousie* was considered a departure from Robbe-Grillet's usual concerns. Although the familiar long, geometrical descriptions of objects appear in the work, the apparent extreme subjectivity introduced by the unusual narrator seemed to contradict theoretical statements made by Robbe-Grillet on the importance of not searching behind the surface of a literary object for its true meaning, which was that surface itself. Up to *La Jalousie* it was assumed that Robbe-Grillet's orientation was outward, from the mind to the world of things. The descriptions in this novel, however, were far from uncontaminated by a subjective consciousness. Yet that subjective consciousness was unemotional; the absent *je* seemed inhuman; and *La Jalousie* was a complete failure when it appeared. Robbe-Grillet was becoming known as an unreadable writer. In his theoretical articles around this time, Robbe-Grillet was suggesting that a new way of reading texts had to be found, a new kind of reader developed. By 1970 *La Jalousie* had become a classic. It was translated into twenty languages and used in textbook editions to teach French all over the world. According to Robbe-Grillet it would be possible for him to live modestly on the royalties from this book alone. A new reader had developed.

Chapter Five
Dans le labyrinthe

Dans le labyrinthe is the last novel of Robbe-Grillet's first cycle
of novels, but it is also a transitional novel, pointing the way
toward the type of writing which would prevail in his subsequent
works. Jean Ricardou has said that *Dans le labyrinthe* is the first
of Robbe-Grillet's novels to reintegrate metaphor, which had
been so strongly rejected in his theoretical writing.[1] This metaphor in its simplest sense links the complex, repetitious trajectory followed by a lost soldier wandering through a strange town
to the process of writing itself. Bruce Morrissette has shown in
detail that *Dans le labyrinthe* is the story of an author's mental
trajectory, his manipulation of his basic working elements into
a story which in this case includes all the drafts made of the
story, all the tentative resolutions the author normally considers,
rejects, and then eliminates from the text. The writing of such
a novel on this subject logically follows the work Robbe-Grillet
had been doing and the concerns he had displayed in his previous
work: a detective story with no crime, a sex/murder story with
no sex or murder, a love story with no narrator/lover, then the
story of the writing of a story.

Unlike the situation in the earlier novels, however, the novelistic, storytelling devices which capture the reader's interest are
minimal in *Dans le labyrinthe*, where there is no compelling mystery, love affair, violence, or sexuality. Character development
is sketchy and yields no insight into human psychology or human
fate. Instead the whole thrust of the novel is to captivate the
reader by showing him the bare bones that Robbe-Grillet puts
together to form a structure which is compelling in and of itself
and which refuses reference to the world of novelistic action.
Thus, as in a labyrinth, the writer tries out one path of thought,

finds that it leads nowhere, opens up no possibilities for development; he retakes the scene, repeats it with slight changes, or abandons it and picks up threads left dangling from other tentative beginnings, whence the exclamation "Non" at several points in the text.

The plot of *Dans le labyrinthe* is minimal. Beginning with contradictory statements about the weather outside, the first section of the novel describes a room to which the narrative will return throughout the novel and in which there seem to be embryonic forms of all the elements which will go into constructing the novel. The narrator is safe in his room. Outside, he says, it is sunny. Then he says it is raining, and finally he settles on the weather he wants: it is snowing. There follows a description of the inside of the room—the fireplace, the chest of drawers, the work table, the table lamp, the dust covering the surfaces of the furniture and the floor—where the narrator is perhaps stretched out on a bed. When the narrator comes to his description of the curtain-covered window, the narration slips back outside where a soldier carrying a box is leaning against a lamp post in the deserted snow-covered streets.

The second section of the book begins with a description of a painting hung above a chest of drawers in the narrator's room and depicting a café scene. The painting is entitled *Defeat at Reichenfels*. In the foreground a young boy is sitting on the floor playing with a box; behind the boy are groups of men sitting around tables, standing at the counter, or reading a notice posted on the wall; a bit apart from this animated scene there is a table with three soldiers sitting motionless. As the description continues, the painting suddenly becomes a real scene. Customers leave the café and the bartender begins to close up; the boy and one remaining soldier begin talking. Then the scene changes to the snowy streets outside as the boy now leads the soldier to this very café.

In the next section the soldier is outside trying to find the street where he was to meet someone. Thinking he hears a voice coming from one of the buildings, all identical to each other, he enters the darkened hallway into which the boy had seemed to disappear earlier. A woman opens her door and learns that the soldier is looking for a street, the name of which he is unsure of. She asks him into her apartment and questions a man in another room about the location of the street. In the meantime the soldier looks around her apartment—the fireplace, the chest of drawers, the table—and notices a picture on the wall of a soldier whom he supposes to be the husband of the woman and the father of the young boy who is also in the apartment. The soldier's mind wanders until the woman and the young boy reappear with a man on crutches. This man insists that the soldier is looking for the street where the army barracks is located and instructs the boy to lead him there. The boy leads him to a building at some distance from the apartment where a man dressed in a jacket marked with the insignia of lieutenant takes him to a dormitory. As the tired soldier begins to drift into sleep, he confusedly recalls scenes and events previously described. When he awakens, a kind of doctor accompanied by the lieutenant examines him briefly. He is feverish, but despite the admonitions to remain still and rest in the barracks the soldier leaves, passing on the way out the man with the bad leg who had been in the woman's apartment.

In the street he comes upon a man carrying an umbrella and wearing a ring who seems to be one of the gentlemen described as being in the café in the painting. The gentleman thinks he has seen the man whom the soldier is trying to find and to whom he wants to hand over the box he has been carrying. The soldier tries to find the place the gentleman indicates to him. But when he again becomes lost, he wonders if he shouldn't simply throw away the box. As he tests out whether the box would fit into one of the street gutters, the young boy reappears. The sound of a motorcycle interrupts their conversation and the scene changes to the soldier helping a wounded comrade walk, then to the soldier walking alone carrying the box, and then to a series of quick scenes that combine elements from the past and the present. The noise of motorcycles draws nearer; from around the corner two enemy soldiers appear. The boy and the soldier try to run away but the soldier is hit by a bullet and barely makes it into the hallway of one of the duplicate apartment buildings before collapsing. The following scenes are memories, thoughts, hallucinations of the soldier, who is now in the woman's apartment in bed. The woman explains to him how he was injured and how, with the help of a gentleman wearing a ring and carrying an umbrella who happened to be there and who is a kind of doctor, he was brought to her apartment despite the wishes of the invalid. The soldier describes how he came into possession of the box. It belonged to a comrade, whom he hardly knew but had helped when the latter was wounded. This comrade died in a hospital before the soldier was able to learn to whom he was to deliver the box which he had been given. A phone call from a man who may have been the dead soldier's father brought the soldier to this town in an unsuccessful search for the supposed father. Confused descriptions follow and this section ends.

The next section begins with a first-person narrator again who seems to be the pseudodoctor/gentleman. He describes how he himself took charge of the box after the soldier's death and despite close calls with enemy soldiers on the street brought it from the woman's apartment to his own. He wonders what to do with the contents, some letters from a fiancée, a watch, a ring and a daggerlike object. He then reviews the roles played in this drama by the boy, the false invalid, the café owner in the painting. He finishes with a description of the room, which he then leaves.

Narration

The issue in *Dans le labyrinthe* which has inspired the greatest amount of critical commentary is again, as in *La Jalousie,* the problem of who is narrating the text and whose point of view the narrator expresses. The first word of the novel is "I," the last "me." A few pages before the last word there is a mention of "my last visit." The "I" at the beginning of the text sets the reader into a particular frame of reference for interpretation of the novel. First-person narrative, used here for the first time by Robbe-Grillet, creates a certain intimacy between reader and narrator stemming from the reader's awareness of the complete subjectivity of the text he is reading and yet at the same time based on the reader's willingness to share that subjectivity and to adopt that point of view. This frame of reference is maintained in *Dans le labyrinthe* over a number of pages, the descriptions of the room, the soldier outside, the painting on the wall all being processed by the reader as being some first person's observation directed entirely outside himself but nonetheless subjective. Normally, this framework for reading the text provided by the "I" at the beginning is strengthened and recalled for the reader by further references to the self narrating, in the form of mentions of actions or movements of this "I" if not of reactions or feelings.

In *Dans le labyrinthe*, however, the "I" is not picked up again until the end of the book and the subjective, limited nature of first-person narration is lost somewhere. There is no break in the text at which the absence of this first person introduced in the beginning is noticed; instead, as the number of pages away from the first word "I" increases, that frame of reference originally set up fades until in the second section of the book the reader is suddenly made aware that his original guide for the text has already been absent for quite a while and the reader's frame of reference has automatically shifted to another form, third person narration from the point of view of the soldier.

As long as the point of view is limited to the soldier, this form of narration poses no problem. When the soldier out on the street looks up at the windows of a building, however, the point of view shifts to the consciousness inside the original narrator's room. Thus, the two points of view come into conflict and cannot be reconciled. The reader has "read through" two separate points of view, one after the other, which cannot be blended into one, the consciousness in the room and the soldier clearly representing two distinct centers of perception. These are the two poles between which the narrative slides until, like a new personality emerging from multiple personalities, the phrase, "at my last visit," which begins the last section, gives the reader a new narrator.

In order to impose some coherence on the text, the reader is forced at the beginning of the last section to rethink the entire book in an attempt to integrate this new first person into the text. This new "I" shares some of the traits of the doctor who helped carry the soldier to the woman's apartment; he also has characteristics of the bourgeois gentleman signaled earlier in the café and then in the street who seemed interested in the soldier. If this "I," the bourgeois gentleman, and the doctor are one and the same person, what is their relationship to the first-person narrator at the beginning of the book? What explanation can account for the descriptions of the soldier's dreams, deliriums, thoughts, all of which this first-person narrator/bourgeois gentleman/doctor could not have been aware of? The standard, and ultimately most logical and reasonable, explanation takes this narrating core to be a writer interested in trying to recreate the events leading up to the death of a soldier.

But just as a logical chronology could not be established for *La Jalousie* and just as the guilt or innocence of Mathias in *Le Voyeur* is not verifiable, so there is a persistent ambiguity built into *Dans le labyrinthe* which argues against the simple reduction of the text to the story of a writer writing a story. Although this reduction neatly explains the diegesis of the text, at the same time it eviscerates its radicality and stops short of dealing with the operation of the narrative. It would be unfair to imagine that Robbe-Grillet's enterprise here was simply to come up with a story, the ambiguity of which could be explained away once the key to interpretation is revealed and the "real" story extracted from the overlaid text, like the baroque paintings which revealed hidden images only when viewed from a certain angle. In his discussion of the new novel Stephen Heath criticizes traditional reading's continuous attempt to arrest the circulation between sign and meaning, to find the key which will explain away all ambiguities, and to reduce the text to one single truth: ". . . the text is . . . consumed, the story extracted, the production ignored. Such consumption is in Robbe-Grillet's terms an operation of recuperation and it is precisely this consumption that *Dans le labyrinthe* aims to distort. Robbe-Grillet projects the accomplishment of an irrecuperable text."[2] Rather than seeking a way out of the labyrinth, the reader is asked to take pleasure in the very structure of the labyrinth.

The Life of Forms

The labyrinth is made possible by the similarity among the objects described. Each single object in the text shares traits with other objects, implying at the same time noncoincidence with itself and unity with the other, a unification of the diverse. *Dans le labyrinthe* represents a hesitance between unity and diversity, or rather a refusal to label existence. Thus, in the narrator's room, which is almost a duplicate of the woman's apartment, there is a box which may or may not be the one the soldier is carrying, which may or may not be the one which the boy is playing with, either in the woman's apartment or again in the painting on the wall. The refusal of any one narrative element to remain coincident with itself coupled with the tendency of all the narrative elements to merge into union with others gives Robbe-Grillet's novels their characteristic aura of movement going nowhere, of "fixed vertigo," as Gérard Genette calls it.[3] This static movement is supported temporally by one of Robbe-Grillet's privileged words, *maintenant,* a time expression which in Robbe-Grillet's works invariably functions to eliminate any time but that of the reading of the text.

The objects which participate in the double movement of merging then splitting apart are introduced and begin to proliferate, generating links among themselves in the first section in the novel. The dust in the narrator's room falling slowly onto his table like the snow falling outside retains traces of basic, simplified, flattened contours of objects in the room, the forms of which will reappear throughout the text: "A circle, a square, a rectangle, other less simple forms, certain ones partially overlapping, already blurred, or half erased" (10).[4] The objects suggested by the traces must now come into being in the text: the soldier's box, a dagger, wine glasses, a desk lamp. The lamp inside the room, echoing the street lamps outside the room, casts an incomplete circle of light against the ceiling and one wall covered with a curtain instead of wallpaper. The curtain is drawn, separating the inside from the outside. But the curtain's separating function is at the same time a linking function, at once covering and indicating the passageway between the inside and the outside.

Thus, each time curtains are mentioned a shift can occur between inside and outside. The curtain also negatively introduces the wallpaper in the room, missing from the curtained wall but present on the other three. The wallpaper carries a cross-shaped motif which echoes a cross-shaped form in the dust on the table. In the initial descriptions of this cross-shaped form in the dust there was some hesitation, a few false starts: was it to be the figure of a flower, a human being with his arms stretched out, or a dagger? The last, most evocative and dangerous interpretation of this form is retained. "A similar design still decorates the wallpaper . . . a flower, a kind of clove shape, or a tiny torch, whose handle is made up of what was just a minute ago the blade of a dagger . . ." (20). These similar figures overlap and refer to each other so that the dagger Robbe-Grillet had settled upon as the cross-shaped object becomes the figure on the wallpaper.

In order to expand further the implications of the form within the context of the novel, Robbe-Grillet makes one more switch; from a torch with a flame, the figure on the wallpaper becomes an electric torch, thus converging with the lamp in the room and the lamp outside. This link is particularly important because it permits reference to "the man"[5] standing outside near the lamp post. The link that occurs at this point between the cross-shaped form which is a dagger—a link made possible by the movement from the wallpaper to the lamp to the circle of light cast on the ceiling and the curtain which transports the narration to the outside—and the man standing in the snow outside near the lamp post causes the image of the man to solidify, and he becomes a soldier. The interplay and the reciprocal influences among the elements of the novel make the transformation inevitable. The presence of the man had been signaled earlier by the mention of the footsteps heard outside, "the sharp clicks of iron tipped heels on the pavement" (12), and even in the first sign of movement the "sharp click" (*bruit saccadé*), a noise associated with a machine gun, and the "iron tipped heels" suggest a military connection. The suggestion of the military in turn has an influence upon the choice of meaning to give to the cross-shaped form in the dust. When the form becomes a dagger-bayonette the range of possi-

bilities narrows and the man in the snow inevitably becomes a
soldier.

Like planted seeds, the figures in the dust generate suggestions
for new similar forms. The soldier carries a box under his arm
in a sense because on the table in the narrator's room a rectangular
shape in the dust came to fruition. The dagger image fixes the
soldier's identity and at the same time is no more than one
possible elaboration of the cross shape, reiterated in the string
tied in a cross around the box. The same generative or at least
suggestive capacity exists at other levels. As the soldier notices
a slight opening in a doorway, he or the narrator comments on
the size of the opening: "wide enough for a man to slip through,
or a child at least" (23). The mention of the possible existence
of a child is repeated in the same terms a few paragraphs later,
this time once again in negative terms: "And the whole scene
remains empty: not a man, nor a woman, nor even a child" (25).
Thus, denials of existence are announcement of existences to
come, reverse introductions to the players or objects in the action.
Each time a list of alternatives (". . . there are several dark
smears which could be traces of fresh mud, or of paint, or of axel
grease" [23]) or of negative alternatives ("not a man, nor a woman,
nor even a child") occurs, each of the elements mentioned has
the potential of blossoming into a diegetic or a narrative element
which may play a role in the text. Thus, with the second negative
mention of a child the reader is being prepared for the presence
of the child in the same way as shortly after the mention of
"paint" the painting appears: "Just above is hung the painting"
(24). Again as with the first mention of the soldier, the definite
article is used, indicating that the reader was to have been ex-
pecting a painting given the elements in the text which had been
announcing its arrival.

The Painting

Once the painting appears in the text it becomes the focal
point of the elements which go into making up the action of
Dans le labyrinthe. That is, the objects, forms, and persons mentioned before the introduction of the painting must be integrated

into the painting as elements of the café scene. Moreover, elements which appear in the painting must in turn be integrated into the framing narration. Robbe-Grillet's use of the still shot in the form of this painting is far more complex in *Dans le labyrinthe* than it had been in his previous works where the technique nonetheless did appear. In *Les Gommes,* Garinati freezes on his way up the stairs of Dupont's house; stopping the action in this way had the effect in *Les Gommes* of denaturalizing the actions of Garinati, of destroying the novelistic illusion of reality. In *Le Voyeur* the picture of Violette/Jacqueline helped to actualize Mathias's fantasies by providing a point of convergence for all the vague suggestions of sexuality and violence he had experienced. In *La Jalousie* a picture of A... which also shows the arm of her husband in one corner reminds him of her absence on the night of her trip to town with Franck and reminds the reader of the peculiar status of the husband, never really quite present himself.

In *Dans le labyrinthe* the painting serves with the narrator's room as a kind of generative center. Two narrative spaces, the narrator's room and the streets outside, had been set up; a third is introduced with the painting and this space is a particularly mobile one. In opposition to the stillness of both the narrator's room and the labyrinthine, snow-covered streets of the city, the painting depicts a scene of great animation and excitement. It is in the nature of a painting representative of reality to capture and freeze that moment in immobility; yet not only does the painting portray more movement than either the narrator's room or the outside streets but the painting also actually comes to life. Furthermore, up to the point in the text of the introduction of the painting, the forms described inside the narrator's room are empty of meaning; the squares, circles, and spirals leave little room for interpreting and cannot readily be combined into a story. With the introduction of the painting, a story becomes possible. The painting offers the link between the inanimate objects described in the narrator's room and the possibility of animation suggested by the presence of the soldier on the street but theretofore unfulfilled.

The first description of the painting is preceded by an introduction evoking its opposite. In the "other" space of the book,
the narrator's room, there is no possibility for action: "And the
whole scene remains empty: not a man, nor a woman, nor even
a child" (25). The still painting paradoxically provides the element missing from the narrative up to this point, the possibility
of action in the form of people: "The painting . . . represents
a cabaret scene. . . . A large number of people fill the whole
scene" (25). This entire section of the book consists of the narrator's appropriation of the elements present in the painting. The
narrator takes possession of the scene first by describing it, im-
posing only very tentatively any meaning on the fixed situation
present before him or on the gestures of the actors "no doubt very
expressive. . . . They . . . are making exaggerated gestures
and violent facial contortions, stopped dead in the middle of the
gesture, which makes the meaning also quite uncertain, especially
since the words yelled out from all over have been absorbed as
if by a thick glass wall" (26). This last reference to the glass wall
begins the integration of the painting into the narrative by recalling the heavy curtains that at once separate the narrator from
his story and allow him access to it. Furthermore, the position
of the narrator on one side of the window (i.e., the glass of the
picture frame) through which he watches the café scene links him
to the soldier who will later be in precisely the same position
outside the café looking in through the window. This superim-
position of the narrator upon the soldier in a kind of flash forward
blurs the distinction between the two making recuperation of the
text as the story of the writing of a story just a bit less possible.

The interplay between the narrative and a painting which the
narrative describes and which would normally be supposed to
exist separate from and prior to the narrative is at its most complex
in terms of the characters playing roles in the action. In the
chronology of the text only the soldier existed prior to the painting, although the existence of both a child and a woman had
been suggested earlier. The child actually appears for the first
time in the painting. More importantly, the one character who
has no role in the narrative whatsoever until he becomes animated

out of the painting is the gentleman drinking at the counter whom the solider meets later in the street and who becomes the pseudodoctor at the end. This pseudodoctor also appears to become the pseudonarrator at the end through his appropriation of the two first person pronouns. Thus, the paradoxical interplay between a presumably preexistent text, the painting, with the written text in the process of forming itself is complete; the narrative both creates the painting and is created by it just as the painting, whose existence depends entirely on the text, is at first described as if it were preexistent to the text.

Once characters are introduced they are able to push forward the development of the novel. In *Dans le labyrinthe* they often do so by failing to interpret correctly what they hear or see. This failure to understand results in the character's postulating a series of possible meanings for what they perceive, a process similar to the one the narrator uses, for example, when he tries to organize a simple cross-shaped figure in the dust into a meaningful image of an object. The feverish soldier cannot understand clearly what people say to him; the words are confused, they are spoken too quietly, or they simply fade away before he is able to interpret them. Language is reduced to vague meaningless fragments, noises in which patterns and distinctions can be discerned but cannot be interpreted, degenerating into intonations and grunts quickly swallowed up by passing time and silence. The soldier's questions are never answered; in addition there is a whole series of questions asked by the boy as well as speculations by the narrator that essentially duplicate the questions which might be asked by a reader searching for a meaning under the surface of the text. The boy wants to know what is in the package, what regiment the soldier is with, where the soldier slept, why he changed coats. Throughout the text, the narrator speculates on what his characters are doing and why: "The soldier must have run into him several times then . . ." (40). "The child then must be looking towards the entrance" (52). But these issues cannot be resolved nor a thread found to lead out of the labyrinth because there is a basic problem with the nature of reality in this labyrinth which precludes interpretation.

Reality presents itself as a series of identical objects, the streets, the rows of buildings, the arrangements of the windows in these buildings, the line of doors along the corridors inside the building. Human beings as well appear in series: in the barracks a double row of soldiers fill up a double row of beds. Like Marcel Duchamps's painting *Nude Descending a Staircase,* the boy who leads the soldier around the labyrinthine town appears to him in a series of flashes as the boy runs away, periodically illuminated by the lights of street lamps he passes and alternately disappearing from sight between the lamps. These flashes of light duplicate the soldier's experience standing in the hallway of the woman's apartment as the timer turns the hall lights on and off offering only disconnected glimpses of the environment, more confusing perhaps than might be continuous darkness, but in any case no more helpful to him than the series of footprints in the snow leading nowhere and everywhere at once.

Dans le labyrinthe is a study of the creation of a fiction, but not necessarily the fiction of a narrator who can also be pinpointed as a character in the text. In a foretaste of his novels to come, in *Dans le labyrinthe* Robbe-Grillet allows several narrators to narrate; that is to say, the point of view centered on the "I" mentioned at the beginning of the text is appropriated by the soldier over the length of the text and then taken over by the doctor at the end. Because of the number of narrators there is a proliferation of fictions. In addition to remembering, describing, and distorting real scenes, the soldier, confronted in the woman's apartment with a picture of a soldier, creates a fiction to explain the picture. In so doing he links elements of the picture—the house seen in the picture behind the man, the man's uniform, the pose he takes for the picture, his apparent age—with elements of the reality surrounding the soldier himself—the woman, the boy, the apartment, the neighborhood. The links the soldier creates are the same kinds of links that the text itself makes between the soldier in the apartment, the soldier standing under the street lamp, the soldier sitting in the café, and each of the elements of the text. On one level *Dans le labyrinthe* is the story of the soldier's wanderings through a city; but in addition it is the trajectory of each element of the fiction through the text, the animation and displacement of persons, objects, and gestures in silent spaces, these spaces, objects, and trajectories holding for the reader "neither more or less meaning than in his own life, or his own death" (Preface).

Chapter Six

La Maison de rendez-vous

After the appearance of *Dans le labyrinthe,* it was six years before Robbe-Grillet published another novel. In the meantime he had produced two movie scenarios which brought to fruition preoccupations and interests already hinted at in *Dans le labyrinthe.* These same themes reappear and are fully explored in *La Maison de rendez-vous* (1965), a book which marks a sharp break from his previous works in tone and subject matter, a clear change in orientation, continuing the literary concerns apparent in the earlier works but now reflecting a new level of consciousness in the author.[1] The impetus for this change of direction came from several sources. On one hand Robbe-Grillet had been distressed at the quick recuperation of *Dans le labyrinthe* a few years earlier. Whereas he saw *Dans le labyrinthe* as a book in which narrative problems and structures were of foremost importance and in which the anecdotal elements were reduced to a minimum, many readers ignored its most modern aspects and found in it the symbolic representation of man's search for God. In addition, always sensitive to the development of theory of the novel, Robbe-Grillet discovered in Jean Ricardou a theoretician whose analyses of literature, including his analysis of Robbe-Grillet's own work, helped him better to understand the processes he himself had already used but for which he had not yet developed the theoretical underpinnings. Not since Roland Barthes's articles on Robbe-Grillet's "objective" literature had a critic been able to contribute so much to his work. Finally certain techniques which Robbe-Grillet had been able to explore in the two films, *L'Année dernière à Marienbad* and *L'Immortelle,* changed his perception of what was essential in his work; he found, for example, that he was not at all interested in objects. Whatever shots of isolated objects appear, for instance, in *L'Année dernière à Marienbad* were introduced by director Alain Resnais and not Robbe-Grillet.

La Maison de rendez-vous is an expression and a solidification of two themes which had appeared in the earlier works but which were to become the focal point of Robbe-Grillet's experiments on the novel after 1965: on one hand, the invention of fiction, i.e., the imaginative generation of forms within the text based primarily on textual considerations, and on the other, cultural stereotypes, particularly the exploitation of the expressions of erotic impulses in modern society. Gestures, photos, cultural cliches are generators in the text. Robbe-Grillet's discovery that objects per se do not interest him also caused a noticeable shift in emphasis in the novel away from the description of isolated objects that had become the most readily recognizable characteristic of Robbe-Grillet's style. Instead of a limited number of objects without meaning in themselves described in geometrical detail of lines, spaces, and surfaces, in *La Maison de rendez-vous* objects or characters are often merely named, and it is the developing associations of these objects and names which form the fabric of the text. For the first time in *La Maison de rendez-vous* Robbe-Grillet systematically quotes his own works in an affirmation of the continuity of his creative production. The narrative voice becomes more ambiguous. The characters are flatter than ever before, resembling superficial cartoon characters. The anecdotal element, reduced to a dry minimum in *Dans le labyrinthe,* is much more apparent in this text, making this book generally easier to read and thus accounting for the relatively quick popular success of this book compared to previous ones. But at the same time this anecdote consists of a profusion of variants impossible to pin down to one reconstructable story. The silent slowness and gravity of *Dans le labyrinthe* give way to *tableaux* in *La Maison de rendez-vous* which arrest activity but then come to life in bursts of adventures. The careful prose of *Dans le labyrinthe* reflecting the concerns of the text in the very structure of the sentences and paragraphs changes pace and becomes at once more transparent, by readily yielding up story sequences, and more opaque through a series of self-references and textual jokes. In fact Robbe-Grillet's sense of humor is so sharp in *La Maison de rendez-vous* that critics who found the work intelligent and ingenious at the same time felt disturbed at its lack of seriousness and its refusal to express human values or to deliver the kind of moral message that, despite Robbe-Grillet's efforts to prevent, critics managed to squeeze out of earlier works.

In an ironic reversal, what had at first seemed so difficult to come to terms with in Robbe-Grillet's work, the seeming gratuity of the long, detailed description of objects, would have been perfectly acceptable here as the development of the theme of eroticism. If a description lingered excessively on a woman's fragile shoe or close-fitting dress, the description could have been immediately and unproblematically assimilated under the rubric of erotic excitation. Yet long descriptive passages are relatively infrequent in the story of the adventures at the Villa Bleue.

This is not to say that the book is easily consumed or recuperated. The unresolved tensions created by contradictions in the earlier books reappear immediately in *La Maison de rendez-vous*. The author's preface is divided into two parts, the first denying, in the style of old movies, any resemblance between Hong Kong and the place called Hong Kong in this book and the second claiming perfect fidelity to the real thing based on the author's years of residence in the Far East. The serious tone of the preface to *Dans le labyrinthe* assigning the book the meaning of the reader's life and death gives way to a flippant play on words making a reference to the Surrealists and to Robbe-Grillet's image as a writer: "Any resemblance to the latter [Hong Kong] in setting or situations is merely the effect of chance, objective or not" (Preface). Announcing in the preface his general program for the book, Robbe-Grillet warns the reader, "things change fast in such climes."

Despite the new emphasis on anecdote, on naming instead of describing, in *La Maison de rendez-vous*, a detailed summary of the tangled action of this book must give way to a description of the main incidents. The opening paragraphs reveal the central feature of the book: erotic fantasies, i.e., the eroticism and the fantasies of a first-person narrator whose identity and location,

as the preface warned they might, "change fast in such climes."
In the first few pages the narrator discusses his fascination for
women, and as he gives an example of the kind of situation which
arouses him, the setting for the narration shifts from generalized
time and space—a narrator "speaking" directly to an audience—
to the description of a specific ball and thus to the introduction
of the "characters" in the book. The main character around whom
most of the narrative turns, and the only one who sometimes uses
the first-person pronoun, is Ralph Johnson, otherwise known as
R. J., or R. Jonestone, or Johnston, or Jonstone, or Sir Ralph,
who is an American, or an Englishman called the American, or
a Portuguese from Macao. The ball is taking place at the Villa
Bleue, a high-class luxury brothel run by Lady Ava or Eva or
Lady Bergmann or Eva Bergmann. In her service is Kim, a Eurasian who may or may not have a twin sister whose name is not
Kim, the reader is told, but may be Lucky. Also living in the
Villa Bleue is a young European woman, Lauren or Loren or
Loraine or Laura, who is perhaps the fiancée of Georges Marchat
or Marchand and who becomes involved with Ralph Johnson.
The diegetic center of *Maison* is the death of Edouard Manneret
or rather the several deaths of Manneret and the events leading
up to them. Manneret is alternately a drug dealer, a dealer in the
slave trade, a writer, an artist, or a doctor experimenting with
various drugs on Kim, who is perhaps his daughter.

The most straightforward movement of the narrative begins
during an evening ball at Lady Ava's. Ralph Johnson arrives early
and takes a stroll around the grounds, where he is witness to
some rather strange scenes involving both characters from the
narrative and statues forming little *tableaux*. When he finally
enters the Villa Bleue, Lady Ava tells him of the death of Edouard
Manneret, something which he already knows but will not admit
to knowing. Lady Ava offers Ralph Johnson, one of her special
guests, the favors of a new girl at the Villa Bleue, Lauren, who
is in mourning for having recently lost her fiancé, Georges Marchat. Ralph Johnson soon finds he cannot live without Lauren
and asks her to follow him to Macao, where he must go to escape
the British police in Hong Kong, who are pursuing him either

for smuggling drugs, for selling young girls into slavery or worse, for being a Communist agent, or for having murdered Edouard Manneret. Lauren, who had been put up to this trick by Lady Ava, agrees to go with Johnson in return for a large sum of money which she wants by dawn of the next day. In search of this money Johnson in vain visits Chinese money lenders in Kowloon. He creates a disturbance in the street and is stopped and questioned by some police officers who appear on the scene. In answer to their questions Johnson recounts his activities of the evening, recommencing the narrative exactly as it had appeared earlier in the text, his invitation to Lady Ava's, his early arrival, his stroll around the grounds, etc. When he finally gets away from the police, he goes to see Edouard Manneret to ask him for the money. In one variant of this scene, Manneret pretends to take him for his own son; in another Johnson shoots and kills him. Having failed in any case to get the money he needs, he goes back to his hotel to get ready for the ball that night at Lady Ava's. This time when he gets there, Lady Ava, who had been perfectly healthy at the beginning of the book, now is old and on her death bed. When he then goes into Lauren's room to get her, he finds the British police there waiting for him.

The second primary narrative line centers around Kim, Lady Ava's Eurasian servant, although this narration always remains in the third person, never shifting to the first-person pronoun even when the narration is clearly centered on this character. She first materializes in the text just as Lauren did, through a generalized description of the stimulus for the erotic fantasies of the first person narrator, and just as Lauren did, she takes shape gradually as a character, beginning with a description of her clothes, her walk, the dog beside her until enough specifics are added so that she comes to life, so to speak, on the streets of Hong Kong. Throughout the book there are numerous glimpses of Kim walking down the street with Lady Ava's vicious dog on her way to see the Chinese money lender, drug dealer, or slave trader or to see Edouard Manneret, but the incidents in which she is involved are linked together much less straightforwardly than those of Johnson.

In Kim's first continuous adventure she goes to see a Chinese
drug dealer to pick up an envelope full of small packets of white
powder. As she arrives at the designated house a problem arises
as to where to attach Lady Ava's dog while she goes inside. This
problem is ignored in a variant occurring immediately after this
first scene in which Kim picks up not a packet of drugs but a
young Japanese girl, Kito. In the following scene in a dungeon,
Lady Ava's dog is instructed by Kim to tear the clothes off Kito,
but as he does, the scene slides into a scene from a play being
performed at Lady Ava's ball. There is a series of short vignettes
involving Kim and her visits to Manneret, who may be her father
or who may also be using her to test out various drugs and their
capacity for inducing her to submit entirely to his control. Kim's
longest adventure occurs on a visit to Mr. Tchang, a Chinese
smuggler. She has a great deal of difficulty finding him since all
the Chinese she encounters look alike and are named Tchang. She
eventually finds the correct Mr. Tchang, who sells her Kito, and
the narrative links up to the scene with Kito described earlier.
At the same time, however, an alternate development is described. She is not looking for Tchang, but for Manneret. She
enters his apartment and finds him dead.

The narrative switches in briefer scenes to the point of view
of Georges Marchat and to Lady Ava. In despair for having been
rejected by Lauren in favor of Ralph Johnson, Marchat goes on
a drinking spree and ultimately is found first dead drunk and
then in a variant scene dead at the wheel of his car. The scenes
focusing on Lady Ava are a mixture of her real actions, her actions
as part of one of the plays put on in the Villa Bleue for her guests,
and finally her thoughts as she inexplicably lies dying and remembers or imagines her youth, her home, and the stories people
would tell her about exotic places she never visited.

Metamorphosis

The description of Lady Ava's thoughts about exotic places like
Hong Kong is an example of Robbe-Grillet's systematic undermining of the narration. One of the few elements of the text that
remains stable is the setting of the action in Hong Kong. Coming

as it does, however, at the end of *La Maison de rendez-vous,* Lady
Ava's suggestions that none of this story is true because she has
never been to Hong Kong so shakes the reader's complacency
about the status in reality of the adventures that some critics,
hoping to account for the contradictions in the text and to force
it into a more conventional mode, have been led to argue that
all of *Maison* is a fragmented story told in an asylum by an insane
old former actress who incorporates elements of plays in which
she has acted into a wild hallucination. But the reader is warned
from the very outset, even before the narration officially begins,
that everything that will be affirmed in the text will sooner or
later be denied by the text. In the prefatory paragraph the author
issues a disclaimer: nothing which follows is true; and on the
next page in the second preface, the author, this time designating
himself as a player in the text as well, that is, as one who lived
through these types of adventures over many years of his life,
insists on the objectively verifiable reality of the adventures to
be recounted in the book. Although the reader might be inclined
to take the first paragraph at face value, the contradictory second
should be sufficient warning of the unreliability of what is to
follow. The final remark in the preface, "things change fast in
such climes," announces the principle governing the construction
and deconstruction of this text, metamorphosis.

In Robbe-Grillet's books before *Maison,* one scene would often
metamorphose into another scene by means of an object present
in both. With *Maison* not only do scenes fade one into the other
by the intermediary of a shared trait but also for the first time
the constellation of traits associated with any given character is
not permanently fixed to the character but rather shows additions,
omissions, and shifts from one appearance to the next. The first
instance of this kind of shift occurs in the blending and then the
separation of the two images of young women. As Kim walks
down the street, the narrator first transforms her clothes into ties
binding her and her movements into a struggle to free herself
and then transforms these movements of the Eurasian girl into
those of the blond European girl at the ball responding to the
lead of her dance partner. Thus, the vaguest similarity of move-

ment allows a shift from one person to another. Furthermore, an occupation, a nationality, a name are not necessarily permanently attached to any of the characters. Ralph Johnson is perhaps a drug dealer, a slave trader, a Communist spy, the murderer of Manneret; but Lady Ava is also perhaps a drug dealer, a slave trader, and a Communist spy. So is Georges Marchat, perhaps. The traits that allow people to be recognized and distinguished from each other become blurred and fluid. Their names change; Johnson, Lady Ava, Lauren, Edouard Manneret, and Georges Marchat all have several variant spellings.

On the other hand, a single name can cover several people, the ubiquitous Mr. Tchangs. Like the myriad interchangeable Chinese under the name Tchang, the name Kim remains constant throughout the text but may designate more than one person. In her first appearances Kim is dressed sometimes in a black sheath dress, sometimes in a white one. Eventually, after the suggestion that the two dresses may be being worn by two different but similar-looking women, the image of Kim does split completely into two and a twin sister suddenly appears. Other duplicates of Kim appear in the form of mannequins and reflections in store windows. All these changes work toward preventing the reader from naturalizing, ignoring, or simply reading through the narrative level of the text.

Levels of Representation

In *La Maison de rendez-vous* Robbe-Grillet makes extensive and varied use of the technique he had developed in *Dans le labyrinthe* by which the painting of the *Defeat at Reichenfels* became animated and descriptions of "real" scenes became frozen and merged into the painting. *Mise en abyme* or internal duplication is used in *Maison* both to anticipate and to repeat "real" scenes: the knick-nacks in Lady Ava's house, the statues in her garden, and the props she stores for her theatrical productions all duplicate characters or actions which appear elsewhere in the text. In addition to the technique of internal duplication, in *Maison* Robbe-Grillet also utilizes a more complex, disturbing technique of continuance of a scene in which, while there is no break in the narration, the level of narration shifts. A good example of this technique appears in the description of the picture in a Chinese magazine swept up by a street sweeper just as Kim walks by him. The picture, ". . . a crude drawing, represents a huge European salon . . ." (19). The details of this crudely done picture are supplied gradually in the description of the picture but with such precision that after a page and a half of description the reader begins to wonder how so much detail can appear in one picture in a magazine.

It becomes more and more difficult to keep in mind that this text is only the description of a magazine picture, partly because of the abundance of detail and partly because of the use of certain words more appropriate to movement than to the description of a picture. One section of the picture shows British police at the door of the salon. "But only a few people have noticed their sudden appearance in the noise of the festivities . . . a recoiling movement affects their heads and the upper parts of their bodies. . . . Everywhere else in the room, local involvements are sustained as if nothing were happening" (20). Tension increases as the reader continues to try to maintain the mental context of the picture in the Chinese magazine until finally movement is unmistakably described: "The young woman, after a few seconds, looks back toward the seated woman" (20). The scene can no longer be taken as merely a picture, and the reader must search for some new context in which to understand this description. Gradually, however, the animated scene reverts to stillness and to the status of a picture, ". . . the rice-straw broom, completing its curving trajectory, pushing the illustrated cover of the magazine into the gutter, whose muddy water sweeps along the colored image swirling in the sunlight" (21). The curve of the movement of the broom and the spiraling movement of the page floating on water offer an image of the curve just accomplished in the narration itself from immobility to mobility and back again.

The introduction of the theme of theatrical representation similarly allows a great deal of flexibility in shifting the levels of narration. In some instances such as in the description of the undressing of the terrorized Kito by Lady Ava's dog, the description begins at the level of narrative reality, but once Kito is completely undressed, there is applause and she takes a bow. The description must now be seen from an altogether different angle; it was only one of Lady Ava's skits. The relationship between these theatrical scenes and the real events always remains ambiguous, with characters within the plays commenting on scenes which take place at other levels. Thus, during one skit, Lady Ava makes comments to Kim about the behavior of Ralph Johnson outside the play. "At this very moment, he must be running around trying to get hold of the money she asked for" (72), and this is exactly what he does. As the scene ends, Lady Ava is about to hide the packets containing the drugs Kim has brought her in Kim's nontheatrical scenes, and the shifting levels of reality are exposed in the narrative in a parody of the causal logic that operates in traditional texts: ". . . if the hiding place was in the room itself, the envelope would have been put away long since, the servant girl has thought, Lady Ava thinks, the red-faced narrator says, who is telling the story to his neighbor in the little theater" (72). This time the status in reality of the preceding theatrical scene is put into doubt as we learn that the fat man is merely telling the story. Was the entire preceding scene only a projection of the fat man's tale filled with stereotypes of the Orient, his "fantastic stories of Oriental travels, with go-between antique dealers, white-slave traders, over-skillful dogs, brothels for perverts, drug traffic and mysterious murders" (73)?

The same sorts of fluctuations among levels of representation occur in the discussions or descriptions of Edouard Manneret; he is killed in the play written by a certain Jonestone, his death is depicted in the Chinese magazine cover, an account of his death appears in the newspaper, and he is said to have been killed, several times over in the course of the narrative, by an unknown assailant, by his business connections, by Ralph Johnson, by Lady Ava's dog, and by Communists. The story of his death is told in detail by the third-person narrator in several versions, ending as a conversation between Lady Ava and Ralph Johnson in which they, like traditional readers of murder mysteries, try to piece together into a logical chain of events all the disparate clues mentioned in the narrative up to that point and at the same time add anything they feel the story needs to be coherent. Like Sherlock Holmes discussing a murder with Watson, Lady Ava suggests that Edouard Manneret's assailant could have been a simple business associate. When Johnson objects to this explanation, she says other versions of his murder could be not logically deduced but rather invented.

Johnson and Lady Ava find "unrealistic" details in the description of Manneret's death: he dies from being accidentally stabbed in the neck by a broken piece of a sherry glass. Hardly likely, they comment, and furthermore, sherry is not served in the kind of glass described. But if the narrative does not fit the logic of the real world, Lady Ava reminds Johnson, "It was all a setting . . ." (125), thus putting the narration back to the level of a fiction within the narration, and the third person narrator resumes his own description referring to the assassin as the stage director who "more concerned with decoration than verisimilitude, . . . also removes the corpse's shoes and puts them back on inversely" (126). The reader is once more reminded that whatever the level the text is operating on at any given moment, all levels are fiction, all of them are designated by Kim's finger pointing to "the verb 'represents' (third person singular of the present indicative)" (46).

The Problem of Narrative Continuity

In the course of the narration at whatever level in whatever person, the narrator frequently hits snags where the text designates itself as such and brings the smooth telling of a story to an abrupt halt. One of the narrator's chores is to make decisions about how to describe settings or actions. When Kim goes to see the Chinese intermediary, the narrator devotes two whole pages to exploring thoroughly and enthusiastically the various possibilities of the trivial question of how to handle Lady Ava's dog, where he should be tied up to wait for Kim. But toward the end of the book the narrator seems to reach a point from which he is unable to continue further. Most of the narrative lines have already been played out and the narrator has nothing left to do but continuously to repeat the same sequences or to bring the narration quickly to an end. Exploring all variants begins to become tedious and as the narrator comes to passages in which he must decide whether a door is open or closed, whether the door is later opened by Manneret, Kim, or no one at all, whether Manneret is asleep or awake, he becomes exasperated, "What does all that matter? What does it matter?" (151).

The greatest disruptions of narrative continuity are the periodic references to King Boris. A Boris-like character, Bona, appears as leader of the assassins in *Les Gommes,* and in Robbe-Grillet's first text, *Un Régicide* (not published until 1978), the protagonist's name is Boris. Boris's function in *Maison* is ambiguous. Although all the characters in the text refer to him with familiarity, the reader never has any explanation of who he is or what connection he may have to the actions described. Some of his characteristics overlap with those of Edouard Manneret and at one point Manneret sarcastically says that he is King Boris. Boris manages to intrude into conversations between characters in the text. His interventions become more frequent toward the end of the text. In his first intervention he is said to be searching through his memories; given what follows, references to the bicycle from *Le Voyeur,* to a man in dark glasses with a dog who appeared in Robbe-Grillet's film *L'Immortelle,* to the curtains from *Dans le labyrinthe,* to the gardens from *L'Année dernière à Marienbad,* to the venetian blinds from *La Jalousie,* and to the debris floating in the canal from *Les Gommes,* the implication is that he has some knowledge of other texts by Robbe-Grillet. This series of references ends with the introduction of the cover of the Chinese magazine which eventually becomes a major source of subsequent narrative structures. Thus, King Boris seems to be connected in some way to the writer's creative imagination. Edouard Manneret, with whom Boris is linked, is, at least in some parts of the text, a writer. Furthermore, some stains which Boris makes on the ceiling of Lady Ava's bedroom inspire her to fabricate stories about the exotic East (134–35).

Boris's major interruptions of the narrative voice occur at three points in the text and each time his intervention is associated with résumés of narration, the first time (16) with the catalog of items which appeared in Robbe-Grillet's earlier works, but the last two times, in the last third of the book, with résumés of action in *Maison,* as if Boris, already associated with the creative imagination, were giving the narration a necessary push, an infusion of energy necessary to continue. The second intervention occurs as a first-person narrator begins once again another résumé of Ralph Johnson's adventures. But Boris becomes impatient and puts an end to this tedious repetition by tapping on the floor with his metal-tipped cane, a tap which becomes more rapid as the text approaches its final sequences. Boris's last interruption of the narrator again seems to come to the rescue of the text. At this point a scene is being described which appears for the first time in the text; a woman is described first catching fish to present to diners at a floating restaurant, then guiding a sampan. But the narrative has gotten off the track onto this new subject, which cannot be taken up and developed so late in the text when nearly all other narrative pathways have been explored. The narrative loses its smoothness and replaces description with *etc.* "Returning to shore on a lantern-lit sampan rowed by a slender girl in a close fitting dress, etc., with a gait both provocative and reserved, etc., etc., who manipulates the long gondolier's oar with grace and skill, making undulating movements that slide the thin, shiny silk over her skin . . . (that's enough, up there! the sound of steps, and the iron-tipped cane which repeatedly pounds the floor . . .)" (144). The girl, the sampan, and the restaurant disappear and Sir Ralph's adventures continue on smoothly to the end of the book. Boris's insistent rhythmic tapping thus stops what may have been an irrelevant erotic reverie and puts the narrator back on track.[2]

Stereotypes

When *Maison* first appeared it was hailed by some critics as a brilliant construction but criticized as unfortunately lacking any redeeming social value. There was too much humor, too much tongue in cheek for *Maison* to be considered a serious work. Worse, some critics were incensed that Robbe-Grillet, who had theretofore been regarded as a serious writer, now seemed to be publishing pornography in the guise of experimental fiction. Suspect already because of *Le Voyeur,* Robbe-Grillet was clearly projecting his sexual fantasies into this book and was identifiable as the "I" on the first page; the beginning of *Maison* has even been called a confession.

In response to these attacks against his interest in eroticism, an interest which was to continue to manifest itself throughout his subsequent books and all his movies, Robbe-Grillet began to analyze and elaborate his idea that man's fantasies are no longer personal and internal, but rather they are literally spread out before him in the hallways of the subway, in billboard posters, on television. If he chose to describe Hong Kong, and if "everybody knows Hong Kong" (2), it is precisely because Hong Kong functions as a stereotype, as a locale for the collective unconscious, as a point of convergence for erotic, exotic, and criminal fantasies, from the elegant Asian women in their slit sheaths to Communist agents from Red China, to drug smuggling, cannibalism, luxury brothels, murder, and inscrutable Chinese. Robbe-Grillet feels that this sort of popular culture, the kind found in third-class pornographic novels, is important because it speaks to man of his real concerns. The eroticism in *Maison* grows out of the very first few pages. The first line, "Women's flesh has always played, no doubt, a great part in my dreams" (1), establishes the link between flesh and dreams, eroticism and imagination. Robbe-Grillet has often said that what distinguishes man from animal is man's ability to fantasize. "No bull, however deprived, will let its gaze be attracted by the photograph of a cow's rump. Man is fully human only if everything passes through his head, even (and especially) sex."[3] Robbe-Grillet often quotes the Kinsey Report's conclusion that "the more advanced a man's intellectual values, the more he tends to attribute an importance to the imaginary activities which accompany the real ones."[4] Thus, for Robbe-Grillet intellect, imagination, and eroticism are inevitably linked and the reverie engendered by popular images is a tribute to the creativity of the erotic imagination. The essentially creative impetus stimulated by these insistent reminders of sex endows the narrator with the power to organize, to reign over, to order orgies such as those proposed in the Villa Bleue.

There is an unmistakable violence associated with this power. The fragile skin of the women is juxtaposed against the stereotyped images of chains, whips, and dungeons. Even the innocent straps on the woman's shoe become transformed into leather ties strapping her down. Civilized, displaced erotic activities are described in terms which reveal their origins in erotic ritual: the male dancer merely watches as his female partner displays before him her ability to obey, to follow his slightest movements, ". . . continuing to observe the complicated laws of the ritual, then at an almost imperceptible command, smoothly turning around, again offering her shoulders and the nape of her neck" (2). The emphasis here on the woman's submissiveness and vulnerability regulated by the rules of ritual suggest the dangerous, violent aspects of the erotic imagination.

For the most part, however, in *Maison* this violence is never realized. However fragile the skin on these women is, it never bears the trace of whips, chains, or the rest of the arsenal of torture devices. As a reminder that fantasy is not the same as action, that fiction is not real life, the women in *Maison* have a fluid status in reality, transforming when necessary into mannequins (Kim), actresses in plays (Kito, Lauren), or pictures in a pornographic magazine (Kim). This transformation to avoid violence is used frequently in *Maison*. As the narrator focuses insistently upon the slit in the traditional Chinese sheath dress, the slit suggests a zipper, the zipper opens revealing the naked flesh beneath, and suddenly the woman being described is no longer walking down the street, but instead is described writhing, trying to break free from bonds. But no less suddenly, as this image begins to go too far, the writhing of the bound woman is superimposed upon the rhythmic movements of the civilized, public form of erotic excitement, the dance. Civilization maintains a safe outlet for erotic impulses and the danger is defused. By the same token the terror provoked by the setting and the situation when Lady Ava's dog is commanded to tear the clothing off Kito is completely dissipated when this scene is transformed into a scene in one of the skits at Lady Ava's ball. Culture comes to the rescue.

The emergence of eroticism as an important feature of Robbe-Grillet's novels after *Dans le labyrinthe* can be seen as Robbe-Grillet's desire to "speak" the world around him, that is, to control and manipulate fragments of popular culture, the language of the collective unconscious, so that man becomes not the slave of these images, a role of which he is ashamed, but rather the master of them, confronting them and selecting from among them those which give pleasure.

Chapter Seven
Projet pour une révolution à New York

Projet pour une révolution à New York (1970), although published a full five years later, clearly grows directly out of *La Maison de rendez-vous,* showing Robbe-Grillet's continued interest in the same themes and techniques for narrative development.[1] Once again the flat, colorful projections of our world's fantasies and its images of itself contribute the elements to be arranged according to a logic internal to the fiction. This time the setting is not faraway exotic Hong Kong or a tropical colonialist plantation, but rather, faraway New York, "an imaginary city if there ever was one,"[2] a city of violence, sex, crime, terror, and revolution, a city built on a bizarre, terrifying subterranean world of dark subway corridors, the scream of subway trains peopled with maniacs of all kinds and decorated with incomprehensible streams of posters like the advertisement described in *Projet* for a detergent depicting a woman in a bath of her own blood. This is the New York of nightmares, the modern Western capital which embodies the defeat of humanism, of humanity, and replaces it with mannequins, masked figures, and nightmarish creatures, all victims or victimizers under the relentless surveillance of an all-powerful, inescapable Organization, whose goal is Revolution and whose methods are interrogation, rape, torture, arson, and murder.

But the project of the title is ambiguous and the revolution being prepared is vague. The project is to construct a text, the nature of which is described in the opening lines of the book. The text will be like the projection of a film with rewindings, cuts, and retakes and will engender itself by means of revolution,

96

the revolutions of a role of film or of a cassette tape. The revolution will also be a revolt against the image of the city of New York, against the control exerted by its mythologies of violence and fear. But at the same time the revolution is the continuous textual movement over the same space, an action whose tale is begun by one character and carried along by another and then another to arrive by the end of the book at the beginning of the story in what Jean Ricardou calls an invitation to reread. In several places in the book we read the notation "as has already been said" (183) when in fact it has not already been mentioned, that is, not if the reader is reading the text for the first time. The text demands multiple readings, multiple revolutions of the wheel of the text.

During the period that *Projet* was being written, France was going through the turmoil of its May 1968 revolt and in the United States there were protests against the war in Vietnam. But despite its title *Projet* is neither a chronicle of those events nor a real political statement of any kind. Neither is New York any more the real city of New York than Hong Kong had been real in *La Maison de rendez-vous*. At the time *Projet* was written Robbe-Grillet had spent only a few days in that city. Many readers have noted that cetain descriptions of New York are completely inaccurate: the keyholes in New York are not such that one could look through them; the fire engines do not have the pin-pon–, pin-pon–type siren one hears in France; New York apartment buildings do not have light timers; people use pillows on their beds, not *traversins*. But one need not be a New Yorker to recognize the stereotypes of violence, eroticism, and revolution that invest Western civilization. "The large American city is obviously a privileged place . . . because of the particularly violent mythological charge it carries, as much in the minds of us Europeans as in those of New Yorkers themselves. . . . It represents a paroxysm never before attained of marvels and of terrors, with its underground world of crime, vice, drugs materialized by the immense and decaying underground subway system."[3] Since the title of this book was taken as an advertisement of its contents, some readers and reviewers of *Projet* felt frustrated that the book did not treat social and political issues in the United States in the late 1960s. But Robbe-Grillet has always maintained that the only revolution to which a writer can contribute is not a change in government but a change in the manner of perceiving the world. The title thus forces the reader to come to grips with the idea that a title need not be a straightforward representation of the content of the book any more than the book is a representation of the content of the world.

The content of *Projet* is a tantalizing collection of stories from pulp fiction. The complex, overlapping, intersecting diegesis of *Projet,* weaving together the strands of the events surrounding the characters, begins as though it were the description by a neutral narrator of a projection of a movie; the narrative voice says that a certain scene takes place, followed by a blank, as perhaps a film rewinds, followed by the same scene once again. The frame is thus prepared and the book must now work toward filling in the frame, that is, the length of time between rewindings, with the descriptions of those scenes. In the very first scene a first-person narrator walks out of his house and closes the door behind him; as he does so, he looks back and notices the curved lines formed in the varnish of the wood around a small door window. These suggestive curves begin to take more definite form, generating a second scene, that of a naked woman tied down to the floor in the spotlight of a lamp, her mouth stuffed with a piece of cloth. From a door on one side of the room enters a doctor who seems to be performing some ominous experiment on the girl; from another door enters a tall man wearing a mask followed by a locksmith. The light clicks off as the door clicks shut and the narrator on his own front stairs again wonders if he has left his housekey inside on a chest of drawers. Mention of this chest generates its existence and leads to a description of the inside of the house and of its young tenant, sixteen- or seventeen-year-old Laura, who is waiting for the return of the narrator, alternately her protecting brother and her cruel jailer.

The narrator turns away from the door of the house and spots an obvious stake-out set up across the street to watch him, standing in front of a house which unlike most in the area has no iron fire escape zigzagging down its face, the kind of fire escape which a criminal could climb up to reach a woman's bedroom. This suggestion leads to its own realization—a criminal climbs up the theretofore nonexistent fire excape, breaks a window to get into the house, and rapes Laura. When the rape is over, the criminal character slides back into the narrator, who now appears merely to have been describing all this to his superior, who periodically interrupts the narrator to make objections or to ask for clarifications.

The narrator had left the house to go to a political meeting in a vast secret room in the subway. The subway station is lined with strange slot machines with games based on themes of sex and violence, souvenir shops with plastic reproductions of, among other things, scenes from previous Robbe-Grillet novels, and pornographic book shops. The narrator finds the false storefront he is looking for, that of a false psychiatrist, Dr. Morgan, which allows him access to the meeting. The meeting consists of a staged presentation of the ideology of the color red as the resolution of the basic conflict betweeen black and white, Blacks and Whites. Red is the color of the three primary acts of liberation: rape, fire, and murder; the perfect revolutionary act would combine all three.

Later in Old Joe's bar the narrator converses with two other members of the Organization, Frank, the head of the group, who becomes associated with the interrogating voice, and the Arab Ben Said. The Organization employs a network of spies including call girls and babysitters like the beautiful mulatto JR, who disappeared recently after answering a newspaper ad for a babysitter for a rambunctious thirteen-year-old girl, Laura. JR, or Joan Robertson or Jean Robeson, takes over the narration and describes her first trip to this house, where Laura entertains herself in her guardian uncle's absence by playing cassette recordings of sounds of footsteps on a fire escape coming nearer and nearer, screams, moans, and bits of narrative which overlap with that of the narrator. JR goes to the window to investigate noises coming from outside and sees three people in Central Park below, the primary narrator, JR herself, and Ben Said loading marijuana disguised as Philip Morris cigarettes into one of the Organization vehicles. After completing the marijuana loading, JR goes home to get ready to go out in answer to a newspaper ad for a baby-sitter. In the meantime her executioner, disguised as a policeman, has entered her apartment and is waiting for the appropriate moment to come out of his hiding place on the balcony to torture and kill JR according to the instructions of the Organization. The appropriate moment is after a sexually stimulating "educational" program on TV on ritual sacrifices of young girls in African tribes. The executioner says he will interrogate JR and then set fire to the apartment, from which he flees down the fire escape.

On the street he converges with the narrator on his way home, where he finds Laura reading a detective story he has never seen around the house before. The narrator is upset because, since Laura is forbidden to leave the house, he deduces that someone must have come in to give her this new book. He imagines someone gaining entrance to the house by pretending to have forgotten his keys and calling a locksmith to open the door for him. The narrator leafs through the book looking for the passage which would describe the scene depicted on the cover, a nude woman tied up lying on the floor and a doctor preparing a syringe, and as he skims the book, he comes across the interrogation of JR, a scene begun earlier but never described in detail. The interrogation veers off into a story about Ben Said. One night Ben Said is traveling on the subway and three young hoodlums board his car and plot against him; the adolescents are two boys, M and W, and their gang leader Laura.

The narrator closes the book and gives it back to Laura, who describes an amusing experience she had that day. She noticed that a myopic locksmith had been trying to spy on her through the keyhole and rather than pierce his eye with a knitting needle, she places an illustrated book cover just in front of the keyhole to make the locksmith believe he is witnessing a real scene. The locksmith rushes off to call for help for the unfortunate bound victim in the scene, much to the surprise of the false Ben Said, who is still staked out across the street and who dutifully notes all these events in his notebook. The real Ben Said is still in the subway car, where Laura has just been attacked by a sex maniac, the Vampire of the Subway, disguised as a member of the Organization but really a police informer who is in league with Dr. Morgan. Laura tries to escape them but her route is blocked by a big rat; the villains grab her and carry her off into a secret underground passage leading off the subway tunnel. Laura, Laura Goldstucker, daughter of a rich banker, is interrogated. Dr. Morgan wants her to explain why these hoodlums were keeping Ben Said on the train. Laura tells him that they normally take their victims to the end of the line, where they rob them to buy cassette recordings of frightening sounds, like moans and screams. This is just what they are doing with Ben Said as W leads him out of the subway to a vacant lot surrounded by a high fence covered with publicity billboards. The primary narrator takes over the description of one of the posters which is an exact replica of the front of his house, complete with Ben Said standing guard. The narrator unlocks the door on the poster and steps into a vacant lot strewn with discarded objects from this and from previous and future Robbe-Grillet works, for example, a brass bed, lit up by projector lamps, to which a nude mannequin, who turns out to be JR, is tied. The narrator tortures and burns her in the final act of the interrogation scene that had begun in her apartment.

Outside the fence a locksmith is peering through the keyhole of a door. Seeing the horrible scene on the other side of the keyhole, the locksmith runs off to get help and brings back a new character, N. G. Brown, who happens to be walking down the street in a mask and costume because he is just returning from a masquerade party. Together they go into the house, where they find a girl tied to the floor and Dr. Morgan preparing a syringe, exactly as the narrator had seen as he stared at the varnish on the door of his house at the beginning of the book. The girl on the floor, Sarah Goldstucker, daughter of a rich banker, is about to be bitten by a black widow spider as Dr. Morgan, who recognizes N. G. Brown beneath his mask as a member of the Organization sent to spy on Ben Said, flees out the door, hotly pursued by Brown. Only the locksmith is witness to Sarah's death by spider bite. The locksmith rapes her dead body and then takes off his mask, revealing himself to be none other than Ben Said. In the meantime the man across the street is still taking notes. From here to the end of the book, a dozen or so pages, there is a series of paragraphs, each interrupted by the word "cut," in which the narrator hurriedly connects together various loose ends of the narrative, explaining, for example, how Laura managed to escape from her house, where she was always locked up, to play her role in the subway scene. The last scene, the narrator shutting the door behind him, rejoins the first scenes.

Generation of a Narrative

A text as multiple and slippery as *Projet pour une révolution à New York* cannot be accounted for neatly, completely, and once and for all. The narrative develops through the proliferation of scenes born out of each other and turning back onto each other. First a framework for the novel is established: an original scene takes place in which all the actors play their roles, the narrator says, as precisely as a complex, perfectly tuned machine, each gear putting other gears into motion. The structures and techniques that Robbe-Grillet has developed and explored in his work are all prepared to take a fragment of narrative and to manipulate and expand it into a new creation. So, the narrator asks on the first page of *Projet,* what will this fragment of narrative be? Perhaps a fragment from another complex machine, another novel.[4] *Dans le labyrinthe* ends as the narrator leaves his room, shutting the door behind him. *Projet* begins with a first-person narrator going out of his house and closing the door behind him. Since the person who shut the door behind him in *Dans le labyrinthe* was a doctor, a Dr. Morgan will have a role in *Projet.* The doctor in *Dans le labyrinthe* was also a writer; in *Projet* there will be many references to texts, making reports, taking notes, reading novels, listening to narratives on cassette tapes, the narratives sometimes running parallel to the primary text, sometimes intersecting it and adding elements that have developed within these secondary narratives to the main stream of the narration. The door itself plays the important role of allowing the character to move not only from one room to another but from one narrative space to another; Laura will open the door to a bedroom and walk into a subway car. The window set into this door offers the opportunity to include voyeurism in the text, and since the window is pierced into the door, penetrates it, the idea of voyeurism combines with the notion of penetration to form a rudimentary constellation of sexual aggression.[5]

Robbe-Grillet has often remarked on the human being's incredibly efficient capacity for generating meaning; the mere placing together of two elements is already the beginning of a story. Here the description of the simple act of closing a door that has a window in it sets up many possibilities for recombination. With a nod to Robbe-Grillet's well-established reputation as a writer who gives detailed descriptions which always maintain their focus on the surface of things, the narrator's account of leaving the house begins with the description of the curvy lines made by the varnish on the surface of the door. The spirals on the grill of the door had already paved the way for these curved lines; a second mention of the curves constitutes an insistence and the curves float into the image of a woman. By the time the woman appears, a good bit of the machinery of the text has already been put to work determining paths of development which must be explored in combination with new elements which appear. If someone were to look through the window or through a keyhole, he might witness an interesting scene, provided that the inside of the house is lit. This light suggests interrogation under a spotlight and at the same time theater: thus, disguises, acting, playing, games. Development of the idea of interrogation is reserved for later and the option suggested by the doctor from *Dans le labyrinthe* is pursued. The insertion of a doctor into the story parallels development at the textual level; in this first scene the doctor performs an artificial insemination of the woman which is meant ultimately to result in a birth just as the doctor is inserted into this text to infuse the text with life.

At the end of the first sequence of the book in which the well-oiled machine of narrative development is fed the fuel necessary to bring it into motion, we find that the seminal scene that the narrator had mentioned but could not yet describe at the very beginning of the book has taken place—again: "The whole scene then goes very fast, still without variation" (4). Then like the blank caused by a film or a cassette tape rewinding, a blank space occurs in the narrative, "suddenly the light goes out" (4), and the scene recommences with the narrator once again at the door of his house. All the elements of these kernel scenes will begin to proliferate and recombine; the insemination of the novel form is complete.

Laura's detective story becomes a generator of the text of *Projet* in one of Robbe-Grillet's favorite patterns of textual generation. When the book appears in Laura's hands, the narrator must discover how it got into the house since no one is allowed in and Laura never goes out. Laura lies, explaining that she found the book on the top shelf in the library when she climbed up onto the shelves. Once this explanation is written into the text it is liable to start functioning, producing new textual segments. Forced to accept this explanation as a new given of the text, the narrator wonders why Laura climbed onto the bookshelves and guesses that she may have been frightened by a spider or a rat, perhaps. The emergence of the spider as a textual element had already been prepared: Ben Said, the well-dressed spy, is wearing gloves; the narrator sees an ink blob on the cover of Laura's novel and interprets it as a glove; on further inspection he sees that the glove is really a spider; and finally the spider steps out of the book and retrospectively frightens Laura into climbing the shelves to get the book on the cover of which the spider appears.[6] When the spider's role in the text is complete, it is allowed to return to its source: "The spider . . . leaps toward a corner of the room, climbs from shelf to shelf, up the empty bookcases to the top, whence it had come, and where it once again disappears" (167). But the narrator had offered two suggestions to explain Laura's fright: the spider, already prepared for in the text, and a new possibility, the rat. Having come to the surface in this scene, however, the image of the rat sinks from the surface of the text to join together with other narrative threads subtending the text. Later, when the proper threads are pulled and Laura is frightened again, this time in the subway, the rat floats to the surface as the cause of her fright.

But in the meantime the image of the rat has made other connections with the text. In the first scenes between Laura and the narrator she had complained of hearing noises in the house. Noises become major generative nodes in *Projet,* spreading out into the sounds of screams, gun shots, doors closing, locks turning, subway wheels screeching, glass breaking, and so on, plus the recorded reproductions of all these.[7] The rat links with this series of noises, all of which suggest aggression, when Laura interprets the noises she hears in the house as those made by a rat's nails on the hard floor of an upstairs room, a kind of tapping which at the end of the book transforms into the sound of the footsteps of the police on the pavement and at the same time activates a memory in the reader, the lingering mental imprint of King Boris in the room above Lady Ava's room in *La Maison de rendez-vous.* The narrator had, of course, anticipated this intertextual linkage, but lest the reader miss the chance to make the connection, the narrator addresses the reader directly: "And also: who is tapping in the blind room on the last floor, up at the very top of the big house? You're not going to try and make me believe it's old King Boris?" (178). Since Boris is linked with the creative imagination when he appeared in *La Maison de rendez-vous*, he carries that link with him into this text, and the textual history of the rat in *Projet* becomes an example of how the creative imagination functions.

All these textual links are based on the signifieds, the referents. The object referred to by the word "dresser," for example, might be connected metonymically to such objects as a candlestick and a mirror; as these words appear in the text they in turn bring with them the connections which the objects designated have to other objects in the world, thus enriching the pool of possible narrative elements. But textual expansions based solely on the signifiers exist as well. In a brilliant article on the use of words themselves as generators, Jean Ricardou retraces the development of *Projet* back to its seminal word (not scene or color), "red" (*rouge*).[8] The existence of certain elements in the text can be explained not by what the word means but by the way it is spelled. Scrambling the letters of the signifier *rouge* produces more signifiers, all present in the text: *orgue, rogue, jour, foure, urge, roue, grue, gourd, joue, goret, gré, rue,* etc. The word *orge,* which itself does not appear in *Projet,* nevertheless permits the formations *forge* and *gorge,* both of which do play a role. The series can veer off into variations of one of the words in the chain; thus *rouge* becomes the word *orgue,* which has its own variations: *organiste, organe, orgasme, Morgan, mort,* and *gants.* The connection among the last three in this list is particularly interesting because this system of generators accounts for items in the text which seem to have no other justification. Why is the doctor's name Morgan? The explanation is that this name allows the link among the doctor, death (*mort*), and the glove (*gant*) on the floor near the woman's body which later turns out to be the poisonous spider. In a kind of "overdetermination," as Ricardou calls it, or insistence, the gloves also turn up as a part of the outfit of any well-dressed spy, like Ben Said, or killer who does not want to leave finger-prints. In another link, the gloves suggest the floating hands in the window of a shop selling masks and wigs; and finally, the indefinite shape of a removed glove links with the indefinite shape of a blob of ink squeezed between two pieces of paper, perhaps by a writer, perhaps by the writer of *Projet* himself. Many critics have seen the same kind of playful self-reference in the incident in which JR accidentally burns a triangular-shaped hole in her dress with an iron exactly in the pubic area; this is a burned dress, a *robe-grillée,* pronounced in French almost exactly like the author's name.

Popular Mythology

Nevertheless, although these sorts of plays on words and letters contribute to the multiplicity of possible readings which he is working toward, Robbe-Grillet warns against the assumption that these technical, linguistic manipulations alone can account for his use of various narrative elements. That is, while he agrees that red is an essential element of *Projet,* he does not agree that the idea of orgasm or death, words which form part of one of

Ricardou's linguistic chains dependent on *rouge,* is introduced into the text primarily because their signifiers are similar. To imply that the text emerges primarily from an innocent combination and recombination of letters is to abdicate responsibility for the text and to lay this responsibility on the French language, just as authors had once laid it on the Muses or God or artistic genius. Robbe-Grillet will not allow the responsibility for his work to be assigned to a generative force out of his control. If he chooses rape, murder, arson, and revolution as narrative centers for *Projet,* it is not because the words designating the acts interest him; it is because the role that these acts play in popular mythology interests him. Societies choose certain themes from among all the themes possible in the world and surround themselves with images representing these themes, which become ". . . something like the collective unconscious of the society, that is, the image it wants to project of itself and at the same time the reflection of the problems which haunt it."[9]

As a result of Robbe-Grillet's insistence on these themes, *Projet pour une révolution à New York* caused considerable disturbance when it appeared. On one hand the author was criticized for his perverted interest in sadistic crimes. On the other hand he was accused of refusing to live in the real world, where real revolutions were taking place. The first group of critics closed their eyes to the irony and humor of the text[10] and the second group demanded of the text that it become something which Robbe-Grillet argues no literary text can be. A text is not a commercial product to be consumed like a can of beans, the essence extracted and then the empty can thrown away, but rather a text must be reread, each rereading allowing for different interplays of meanings, that is, different interpretations. Far from being disconnected from the reality of human or social issues, such an attitude toward the creation of forms or of organized patterns must extend into life. The holder of such an attitude never assumes that the world around him can be interpreted only in one way, can never be changed, manipulated; rather he assumes that structures in the world and elements that make up those structures, too, can be manipulated. This is where Robbe-Grillet's political commitment shows itself. He had always taken the position against Sartrean *engagement* that the writer cannot change the world by writing about social issues, cannot fight for the cause of revolution as long as he writes within a system of logic which conforms exactly to the manner of thinking which maintains the old order in place. The revolution must occur in man's thinking.

Robbe-Grillet's erotic or violent games about drug smuggling in Hong Kong in *La Maison de rendez-vous* were far enough removed from his Western reader's experience not to stir up very many real moral objections. With *Projet,* however, Robbe-Grillet began to trample on an entire system of values of Western urban man, playing on his terrors and prejudices, forcing the reader (or perhaps primarily himself) to face his fears, not so that he may come away with the firm conviction that now he must go forth and prevent social horrors, but rather so that he will recognize that these scenes, this violence and sadism, can be manipulated. The reader must see that the myths of sex, violence, crime, and revolution come from fiction, the fiction of comic books or ads for detergent or the fiction of traditional literature, and that these highly charged elements in his life are exploited and maintained by the sellers of perfume and grade-B movies and books. To be unaware or only half-conscious of the source of these taboos is to abdicate one's freedom. The goal of Robbe-Grillet's conscious manipulation of these charged images is to make the reader aware that the value of these images is not inherent in the object but imposed on the subject and to show him that he need not be dominated by the emotions they cause. It is the fact that obsessions are repressed that makes them dangerous; Robbe-Grillet demands that they be devalorized. "This city which was crushing me, I know now that it is imaginary; and, refusing to be alienated and to submit to its demands, its fears, its fantasies, I want instead to recharge them with my own imagination."[11] Rather than allowing the overwhelming city to crush him, Robbe-Grillet chooses to recognize that the city's hold on him is one of mythology, of billboard posters; he too can play the game and control the city by controlling its mythology and using that mythology for his own ends.

Women as Victims

The objection to his work that Robbe-Grillet seems to find
the most difficult to explain to the satisfaction of his critics is
that the victims of aggression are nearly always women. In this
book particularly the function of the women is to serve as the
locale for the playing out of fantasies of love and hate, domination
and submission. Oddly, critics who dislike this book dismiss it
as "a little story of sadists" and critics who take it seriously discuss
techniques of generation and development of themes without
going into much detail about the themes, about the morality of
the themes.[12] Yet these are questions Robbe-Grillet means to
raise. "Constructing a novel is a solitary activity but it is neither
innocent nor cut off from the rest of the universe."[13] Robbe-
Grillet's use of women as beautiful passive victims is, he says,
a parody of the role they play in men's fantasies. But women,
forever the object in a man's world, plays an additional role in
Projet and in many of the films. There are two defense mechanisms
built into Robbe-Grillet's women that protect them from the
hostility of the men. The first lies in their roles as objects; it is
the ability to slip from being women into being plastic mannequins or paper pictures of themselves. This mechanism was
used systematically in *La Maison de rendez-vous*.

In *Projet* a second mechanism develops. Both JR and Laura
save themselves from torture by creating fables. It is the women
who are the fabulators and initiate the fables. Later the stories
are appropriated by the men and the status of the fable is altered.
The fable is no longer just an invention; it becomes the truth.
The men are the holders of truth: "Truth, My One Passion" (83)
reads the emblem on the cap of JR's executioner. This respect
for the truth makes them the protectors of the hierarchy, of the
status quo. The women on the other hand subvert the given
order. JR's executioner comes to her for stories: "And try to
invent details that will be exact and meaningful" (86), he demands. But she does not always recognize which facts are significant, which are useful. Throughout the text the man plays
the role of traditional reader trying to piece together the significant details of the story. The narrator, for example, looks through

Laura's book trying to find an explanation for the cover page; he wants to know the meaning of the scene he sees and what will happen next. Laura's manner of reading is entirely different from his, entirely subversive. She reads from several books at once, picking up and leaving off in the middle of stories: ". . . she mixed up . . . the itineraries of the detectives carefully calculated by the author, thereby endlessly altering the arrangement of each volume, leaping moreover a hundred times a day from one work to the next, not minding her frequent returns to the same passage nonetheless stripped of any apparent interest, whereas she utterly abandons on the contrary the essential chapter which contains the climax of an investigation, and consequently gives its whole meaning to the rest of the plot" (68). But Laura is not interested in having the meaning given to her; she invents her own meanings.

Laura has two interrogation scenes. In the first her interrogator is JR and her narrative is quickly taken over by the primary narrator as if he and Laura were the same character: ". . . the narrator—let's say 'I,' it will be simpler" (57). In her second interrogation by Dr. Morgan, she once again overlaps with the narrator as she explains certain narrative devices such as the use of the word *reprise*. "The reason . . . [is] that you can't tell everything at the same time, so that there always comes a moment when a story breaks in half, turns back or jumps ahead, or begins splitting up" (132). Once again Dr. Morgan plays the role of guardian of the truth. "There will be the report. Your're forgetting that everything is set down there quite exactly, and that no tampering with the truth is permitted" (128). And once again she staves off her torture and death by distracting her tormentors with her stories ("But all this talking isn't getting us on with the job" [130], says Dr. Morgan). The one and only truth which the men seek holds little interest for Laura; it is too limiting. "But for one little truth, there are millions and millions of lies . . ." (51). As Suleiman points out, the subversive nature of her accounts and those of JR earlier is underlined by the appearance only in the narratives of the females of the phrase "And tomorrow the revolution" (91, 133). It is thus the women in *Projet* who are meant to incorporate subversion of the dominant order, revolution, instability, proliferation of possibilities, and imagination.

The Censor

A challenge to the text, and perhaps a built-in defense system as well, is the presence of a kind of narrator's alter ago who anticipates objections to the text that will be made by its readers, demands clarifications of contradictions in the text, and once takes over the narration on his own account. This alter ego can sometimes be identified with Frank, a boss in the Organization (that is, an organizing force in the structure of the text). At times the narrator's text seems to be aimed directly at this questioner as if the text were a report to him. In these cases the questioner is like a stand-in for the reader (or author since the author, too, becomes a reader of his own text as soon as he has written it). But on other occasions, the narrator refers to the questioner in the third person and lies to him. If the questioner's objection is such that it points to an illogical event or explanation in the text, the narrator rearranges the text and adds or eliminates segments to meet the objection to the extent which he feels necessary, which is not always congruent with the logic of the real world.

The final major intervention by the questioner is particularly important because here the questions anticipate the very criticisms that are leveled at *Projet* by its real readers: *Projet* insists too much on sadism and is not an accurate depiction of reality. In answer to the first objection the narrator points an accusing finger at the questioner/reader: "Your untimely questions, which show the excessive importance you yourself accord to certain passages (even by reproaching me for them subsequently) and the lack of attention you pay to all the rest" (162). Furthermore, the narrator claims that this text and all texts are accurate and true: "I am making my report, that's all there is to it. The text is correct, nothing is left up to chance, you have to take it as it is given" (160). But the narrator himself does not have all the answers. "I am making my report," he says; someone else has arranged the events. As a result the narrative sometimes hits snags forcing the narrator to interrupt his account and start again in order to find a narrative path that will lead to an acceptable juncture with another segment of the text. Thus, in the description of Laura in the subway he is forced into several retakes of scenes and in annoyance stops the text short with "No! No! Retake" (120). Like the reader, at the end of the book the narrator is forced to ask himself what role the nurses were to play in the text, and who was Claudia anyway?

The narrator's text is further complicated at a new level as his attempt to interpret and evaluate the book Laura is reading is integrated into his own account. Paralleling the censoring voice that challenges his narration, he draws conclusions about what must be occurring in Laura's book and finds fault with the logic (how can it be that the dark-skinned Sara has blue eyes?); he discovers errors in his interpretation of the picture on the cover of the book (what seemed to be a glove turns out to be a spider). But most interesting, he soon realizes that he recognizes the constituent parts of the scene described at this second level and thus forces the narration to turn back on itself in its duplication of a scene which had already appeared at the first level of narration. The similarities are not coincidences. What the narrator recognizes on page 75 is the text which he himself produced on page 10 and which is its origin. The narrator is reading his own book, and the title page missing from Laura's book reads *Projet pour une révolution à New York*.

The narrator is not the only character who is reading *Projet* and whose reading forms a part of it. Nearly all the characters take up the narrative line in one form or another during the book and seem to have a certain consciousness of what has already occurred in the text, even in the scenes in which they have had no role. Thus, interrogations can be cut off when the story of the character being interrogated dovetails with a story already presented in the text ("All right. We have that passage in the file already" {85}). When Laura becomes annoyed with Dr. Morgan during her interrogation at having to explain the obvious purpose of the retakes, he assures her that he of course understands the purpose but that the explanation is necessary anyway. "I understood. But you had to say it, so that it can appear in the report.—Why bother?—Don't imagine that this report is made to be read by just linguists" (132). A tip of the hat to the reader, and the report also reveals itself to be, like Laura's novel, not simply a *mise en abyme*/internal duplication of *Projet* but the text itself of *Projet* as it unfolds during the reading process. The reader becomes a character in the text as he reads it.

For the most part all narrative threads are tied in the book's coda, illuminating sections of the text that had been obscure or not immediately justifiable. Just as the first paragraph of *Projet* had predicted, after the scenes are played through, a blank occurs as the reader closes the book, turns it over, and opens it again: "And suddenly the action resumes, without warning, and it is the same scene which proceeds all over again, very fast, always just as it was before" (182). The text has come full circle—it is, as one critic calls it, "a revolved project,"[14] and the revolution is about to begin again. This time all the references to the already written report and to the scenes already described will be quite literally references to *Projet*, as the narrator explains in the last words of the text, "as has already been said" (183).

Chapter Eight
Topologie d'une cité fantôme

Projet pour une révolution à New York and *La Maison de rendez-vous* fall into the category of the Nouveau Nouveau Roman, in which the text self-consciously produces itself, in which the process of writing or reading is an important center of attention. With the publication in 1976 of *Topologie d'une cité fantôme*, Robbe-Grillet initiates a third series of new novels.[1] In accordance with his need always to go further than his readers and critics have gone, Robbe-Grillet again produces a text which cannot really be read according to the rules and criteria absorbed from the previous texts. "For me," says Robbe-Grillet, "every new work, every novel and every film is precisely the creation of a new structure. . . . each novel, each film, each work must be the creation of a new form."[2] The narrative themes in *Projet pour une révolution à New York* were stereotypical, flat, comic-book representations of crime, sex, and violence woven together and underlined as parody. Like the work of American pop artists, with whom Robbe-Grillet feels affinity and who have been as interested in his work as he is in theirs, *Projet* was a kind of assemblage of these themes taken directly from our society's discourse on itself as it appears on billboards and in magazines.

The influence of contemporary American art is even more obvious in *Topologie,* especially the influence of collage artists like Robert Rauschenberg. *Topologie* itself is a collage in which the constituent elements are fragments of texts already published by Robbe-Grillet and texts which would be published separately in collaboration with other artists. These texts, interlacing and interdependent, reflect the interlacing strata of the civilizations which the book describes. In *Topologie* we move through five spaces which are really only one space in five temporal transfor-

mations, which include the present, the past of the ancient world,
and a mythological time. But the structures of the eras remain
the same, as the word topology in the title suggests. Topology
is the study of geometrical figures whose configurations remain
unchanged despite transformations of their elements. From ancient times to present in *Topologie* the same buildings, the same
topography, the same accidental objects, the same gestures reappear as civilization after civilization is displaced and submerged.

  Topologie is divided into five sections, corresponding to five
narrative spaces, plus an incipit and a coda, and for the first time
in Robbe-Grillet's works there is a detailed table of contents
including titles for each section. These titles connect the texts
to paintings, collages, or photographs with which they share
certain elements or which were their inspiration and which at the
same time vectorize the reader's understanding of the text. The
Incipit is a reprint of a text Robbe-Grillet wrote for a book done
in collaboration with Robert Rauschenberg, *Traces suspectes en
surface,* in which a first-person narrator about to fall asleep tries
to remember something, apparently after some kind of disaster,
and he describes snatches of scenes: a city destroyed, a nude girl
combing her hair, a prison. In a contrapuntal movement these
flashes melt into a fog and finally reemerge as the word CON-
STRUCTION inscribed on a wall. The narrator is building a
narrative using the debris of time.

  The first narrative, called "Construction d'un temple en ruines
à la déesse Vanadé" [Construction of a ruined temple to the
goddess Vanadis] is divided into seven sections, reproducing the
first seven of ten texts done for a book with Paul Delvaux.[3] The
first begins in the *cellule génératrice* ("generative cell"), a kind of
all-white prison cell for young prostitutes. Sounds are muted,
movements minimal. A sudden cry from outside takes the reader
through the grilled window of the prison into a Greek, Sicilian,
or Near Eastern landscape. A wounded girl, the one who perhaps
cried out, is running along a path away from a temple on the
hill in the distance.

  In another unsituated place, perhaps in the prison, a young
guardian is reading the history of Vanadium to another young

girl, Vanadé. Vanadium, dedicated to the goddess Vanadé, was destroyed in ancient times by a volcano. On the road outside the prison a nearly completely effaced Latin inscription from that time remains, referring to David, the hermaphroditic twin brother of Vanadé. At that time, except for David, the population was all female and reproduction of the species was possible only through a half-homosexual union with David. The story of his birth is told. The all-female town was attacked by enemy soldiers who murdered all the women but one. This one was raped by the soldiers and later gave birth to the demigod David. As the next section of the book begins, the soldiers are described as sailing away and the whole preceding scene overlaps with an identical scene in a play. Near the theater a merchant slices a piece of watermelon for a young mother and her twin children; the little boy's name is David.

The narrative picks up with the play once again and the curtains open on the first scene already described, a prison for criminal young women. One group of women is playing cards. The last card discarded bears the picture of a burning tower, at the top of which stands a young mother and her twin children. The mother takes her two children, Déana and David, by the hand and they begin to go down the tower, down through the building being demolished, past the scenes of the surrounding country-side visible through the windows of the tower, past the prison and the theater, past a museum which seems to house objects left over from previous Robbe-Grillet books, past the initial cell and through a trapdoor into the execution room. Thirty years later David, who is perhaps a playwright, often dreams that he is climbing an endless stairway in an empty house.

The second space is an old empty house. This short text comes from a collaboration with the photographer David Hamilton. It is early morning and David H. walks down the long hallways, opening, one after the other, endless numbers of bedroom doors. Sometimes the rooms are empty; sometimes he surprises a very young nude or half-dressed girl looking at herself in a mirror. The girl daydreams about girls just like her, young with long slim limbs and long hair, in filmy clothes. David H. photographs them.

In the third section, which reproduces the last three of the texts written for Delvaux, the first-person narrator returns. This section is divided into three parts, each describing the ritual murder of a young woman. In the first section the first murder has already occurred and the investigation of it is said to have come to a standstill. That evening the narrator arrives at the theater for the dress rehearsal of the play *David,* where he sees his friend the artist Robert de Berg. The narrator leaves during the rehearsal and walks through the city. In the second section the narrator learns of the murder of another woman which ended the rehearsal of *David* after he had left. In the third section, a guard, Henri Martin, finds the body of the third victim in the crypt of a temple that once stood near the place where an archaeological dig is underway. The police are able to see a pattern in the places where the murders have occurred and anticipate a fourth one in an old empty house to which the narrator then goes to investigate.

The fourth space also comes from the Hamilton collaboration and is divided into two parts, each of which is further subdivided, some of these subdivisions being very short, only a few sentences. There is a new narrator, perhaps one of the girls David H. photographed in the second section or perhaps the girl named Vanadé to whom the story of Vanadium is read; she is locked up in a room of the old house for some fault she is not aware of. The girl daydreams, alone, looking at herself in a mirror, imagining a companion just like herself. They try on romantic, vaporous clothes, tell each other incredible stories, read to each other, and touch each other in an innocent adolescent daydream full of desire.

The fifth space returns to the Rauschenberg text for the first four subdivisions; the last subdivision is a duplicate of the first part of the then-unpublished *La Belle Captive* with paintings by Magritte. In this last "Espace," first-person narration becomes male again. In the first of five subdivisions the narrator awakens from a sleep that may have begun in the Incipit. He remembers some of his actions, which seem to take up where the third

"Espace" of the book left off. In the second section, a girl similar to the daydreaming adolescent is brushing her hair before a mirror in which she can see the reflection of her dead companion, a girl like her, laid out on a low couch. She can hear the footsteps of an assassin coming nearer in the hall outside her bedroom door. The next section quickly reviews spaces described earlier: a landscape, a temple, a crashed car, a goods station, and finally a metal structure with subterranean rooms where the last murder victim was found. In one quick paragraph the major structures in and around the town are described, including its busy streets full of traffic immediately followed by its silent, empty streets. The very last section refers to falling rocks, little waves on a calm sea, a woman's scream, long corridors lined with doors, a murdered mannequin, police, a doctor, a theatrical production which the narrator attends and then leaves to walk around town. In the Coda, the only new text in the book, the narrator is awakened by a cry and his mind wanders in memories and associations as he walks through long corridors.

Origins

Topologie d'une cité fantôme marks a new departure for Robbe-Grillet in which the proliferation of the continuously bifurcating narrative lines of *Projet pour une révolution à New York* and *La Maison de rendez-vous,* in which the narrative formed itself as it went along, gives away to combinations of already existing narrative pieces. Just as theory was catching up with practice and it was becoming possible, thanks to the work of Jean Ricardou and others, to come to terms with a book like *Projet* and to see how the process of textual self-generation worked, Robbe-Grillet's practice shot forward again and "everything soon takes place again as if theory had never been useful for anything."[4] The narrative chunks of *Topologie* are joined by means of elements in one way or another common to the various narratives. The point of articulation may be an object appearing in different contexts in several narratives, such as the couch in *Topologie,* a place of daydreams, of sexual encounters, or of sacrificial offerings. The pivot may be a name taken from the twentieth-century world,

David Hamilton, from the ancient world, the goddess Diana, or from an recombination of letters, Vanada, Diviana, Danae. Or the connection may be topological—the temple on the hill which reappears on a ship's mast or an artist in the prison doing an etching and another artist outside the prison doing a painting as well as the various photographers at work in the text and their models—in which the configurations remain the same while the material varies. The result of these joinings based on some similarity in constituent elements is a literary collage made up of chunks of complete texts assembled in much the way that pop-art collages make use of photos, labels, and newspapers extracted intact from the real world. *Topologie* is a meeting place for extratextual and intertextual discourses.

In this collage Robbe-Grillet even includes his readers and critics. Already in *Projet pour une révolution à New York* Robbe-Grillet had made indirect allusions to the reader through the textually unsituated questioner, who accused the narrator, for example, of concentrating too much on scenes of sex or violence. In *Topologie* Robbe-Grillet plays on the fact that the reader, particularly the reader of the Nouveau Roman, works at developing strategies for reading, ways of processing and linking the information in the text. In a discussion of information theory, Robbe-Grillet pointed out the importance of repetition in a message; it is the redundancy of certain elements of the message that allows the informational elements to be perceived; a pattern must first be established so that deviation from the pattern may become significant, may carry information.[5]

Thus Robbe-Grillet is careful to establish certain patterns—for instance, groups of five. Even before the text per se begins, the reader sees that the book is divided into five parts. In the Incipit the movement toward sleep (signaled by the phrase "Before I fall asleep") occurs five times, as if duplicating the structure of the book. Five of the six walls of the *cellule génératrice* are visible (the sixth being the space open toward the spectator at the theater, if this is a play, or else representing the eye of the reader). There are five rectangular shapes in the cell, four windows and a poster, five rules listed on the posted bulletin, four visible, one masked by a young woman, and five bars over the window, four normal and one broken. When the time comes to describe other furnishings in the cell, the narrator steps in and makes the reader's calculation for him: "According to my calculations and bearing in mind this card, the tableau moving toward its conclusion, and the two wooden tables, there ought to be another rectangle in the room" (20). Robbe-Grillet nudges the reader. The goal of his narrative coincidence with, or at least complicity with, the reader is an acknowledgment of the expectations of the reader, who has learned to look for just this kind of narrative unity.

Finally, with the inscription of the critic and the reader in the text comes the inscription of the writer himself. In imitation of his own movies and the movies of Alfred Hitchcock and others later, Robbe-Grillet writes himself into *Topologie,* and does it in such a way that he purposely disrupts the narration: ". . . the precise meaning of the gestures and objects located in it is not clearly discernible, apparently because of the narrator's head coming right in front, its thick, curly hair obscuring the view" (28). Robbe-Grillet's humorous appearance here is an affirmation of his firm intention to allow no subconsciousness, unconsciousness, or superconsciousness to direct the development of his texts, but to develop them himself, fully conscious.

An enormous number of bits of material taken from nearly all of Robbe-Grillet's previous works, novels or films, appear in *Topologie.* The Greek temple had already made an appearance in *Les Gommes,* along with the description of bits of debris floating in a river. Robbe-Grillet all but gives a footnote reference to *Les Gommes* as the source for the change from the letter G to the letter H on the ship's mast: ". . . although this particular problem— erasing a letter and replacing it by the one that follows it in alphabetical order . . .—was dealt with exhaustively back in the first novel I published" (72). From the collection of stories, *Instantanés,* the first line, "La cafetière est sur la table," ("The coffee pot is on the table"), triumphantly reappears in *Topologie* as "The coffeepot still stands on the table" (99), making simultaneous reference to another critic, Pierre Boisdeffre, and his attack on the Nouveau Roman, *La Cafetière est sur la table ou contre le Nouveau Roman.*[6] The ubiquitous bicycle and the seagull from *Le Voyeur* make an appearance in *Topologie*. Slats are described through which a viewer has trouble seeing as the husband/narrator did in *La Jalousie*. The phrase which appears so frequently in *La Jalousie* and *Dans le labyrinthe,* "Ici, maintenant," is quoted regularly. Henri Martin from *Dans le labyrinthe* discovers one of the murdered women in *Topologie*. From *La Maision de rendez-vous* there are the theater and the anteroom filled with debris from a theatrical performance. Perhaps because it was the book just before *Topologie,* the largest number of intertextual elements comes from *Projet pour une révolution à New York. Projet* contributed situations—a series of doors along a hallway, blood spreading on the floor, a girl listening to the approaching footsteps of an assassin, the narrator's need to hurry to finish the text—and nearly direct quotation—"The dream unfolds in exactly the same way each time . . ." (52).

Finally another group of elements comes from the films: "Et après," the title of one subsection, from *L'Eden et après,* a white car from *L'Immortelle,* descriptions of formal gardens from *L'Année dernière à Marienbad,* and from *Glissements progressifs du plaisir,* a woman's blue shoe, a *prie-dieu,* a mannequin tortured on the beach, an iron bed, the torture of young girls sequestered in dungeons, the prison cell window with four normal bars and one broken one.

The list here is far from exhaustive. Aside from the fact that readers of Robbe-Grillet experience a certain amount of pleasure in recognizing old friends from previous works by Robbe-Grillet, these self-references are not simply a sign of narcissistic self-indulgence. First of all, some of the regularly recurring elements constitute a kind of personal catalog of starred objects, scenes, or expressions for Robbe-Grillet, the centers around which this particular writer's imagination circles. But more importantly each reference to one of the previous works necessarily conjures up the entire work in general or else specific metonymically related parts of the work; for anyone who has read *Le Voyeur,* for example, the mention of a bicycle in a Robbe-Grillet text means the presence of a voyeur. In *Topologie* a bicycle appears in "Quatrième Espace," where the young girl daydreams. The girl had already appeared in "Deuxième Espace" and there she was being photographed by David H.; although David H. does not appear in "Quatrième Espace," he and his spying camera are inserted through mention of the bicycle. Thus, the bicycle brings echoes with it which have the power to force a reevaluation of the text in which it appears.

This kind of self-quoting is more extensive in *Topologie* than it had been in the previous texts but the bulk of self-quotation in *Topologie* is entire texts taken word for word from books published with works of René Magritte, Paul Delvaux, Robert Rauschenberg, and the photographer David Hamilton. The names of the last two even appear in *Topologie:* Hamilton as the hermaphrodite demigod David H. and, in a sexual reversal, as Mrs. Hamilton, the mother of the twins Vanadé or Vanessa and David; Rauschenberg as Robert de Berg, the sculptor and set designer. Robbe-Grillet's first collaborations, reprinted in *Topologie* in the "Deuxième Espace" and the "Quatrième Espace," were published with David Hamilton as "La Demeure immobile de David Hamilton" in the periodical *Zoom* (1970), *Rêves de jeunes filles* (1971), and *Les Demoiselles d'Hamilton* (1972).[7] The texts written for Hamilton draw their inspiration quite directly from the pictures they accompany: blond-haired, barely adolescent girls in sheer, lacy clothes and light wide-brimmed hats looking at themselves in mirrors, lounging half-dreaming among piles of clothes and filmy pieces of cloth, or romping in hazy fields. In fact in Robbe-Grillet's texts the books of photographs and the accompanying text themselves are described, producing a series of *mise en abyme:* "It is a curious book, full of photographs of girls clasped in each other's arms, more or less nude, with their straps always slipping off their shoulders and little knickers that fit loosely between the thighs, the whole thing accompanied by childish captions written in a style that strikes us as being quite out of place" (102).

Robbe-Grillet's next collaborative work, which appears in *Topologie* as Part 5 of the "Cinquième Espace," was part of a text accompanying selected paintings by René Magritte published as *La Belle Captive* in 1975. The artist died in 1967; therefore, this was not a true collaboration. Yet, remarkably, many of the elements of the Magritte paintings fit quite well into the Robbe-Grillet cosmos and reinforce themes Robbe-Grillet had worked with in his earlier works. Bruce Morrissette remarks, "It is as if a surrealist *hasard objectif* brought Robbe-Grillet into contact with the seminal visual image, completley akin to actional thematics already present in his own novels and films: the watching assassin, the murdered nuee [sic] girl, the phonograph, the voyeur spectators, etc."[8]

In Robbe-Grillet's work with Paul Delvaux, the text, which appears in *Topologie* in the "Premier Espace" and the "Troisième Espace," developed according to a process of cross-inspiration, described by Robbe-Grillet in an interview as a dialogue between the two collaborators: "I write the first text, Delvaux answers with an etching which relaunches my own themes and transforms them. I answer in turn with a second text and so on up to ten. The ten stories would be like ten chapters of a continuous narrative."[9] Published in limited edition in 1976, *Construction d'un temple en ruines à la Déesse Vanadé* (also the title of the first subdivision of the "Premier Espace" in *Topologie*) includes Delvaux's etchings of long, thin, expressionless women, mannequins, and statues dressed in light, thin gowns, immobile in stark decors of Greek temples, arches, and columns. Robbe-Grillet's text then is a reverie on these Delvaudian themes filtered through the grill of Robbe-Grillet's own personal artistic interests and obsessions.

But the most satisfying collaboration up to the time of *Topologie* was with Robert Rauschenberg, who more successfully used Robbe-Grillet's texts as points of departure for his lithographs and therefore did not tend, as had Delvaux, merely to illustrate the texts. The texts written for *Traces suspectes en surface* and printed to surround the Rauschenberg lithographs appear in *Topologie* as the Incipit and as parts 1, 3, and 4 of the "Cinquième Espace."[10]

Thus, only two texts in *Topologie* were not collaborative projects. Part 2 of the "Cinquième Espace," called "Cérémonie rituelle," had been written for a Japanese liquor company, Suntory, to appear as a full-page advertisement in a Japanese newspaper. Only the Coda was written specifically for *Topologie*. Thus, in this book Robbe-Grillet's work evolves a new type of intertextuality, not only recalling past works of his own, mentioning objects which appeared there or writing phrases and sentences that echo those in previous works, but here constructing a text with blocks which are themselves entire texts written under separate inspiration by paintings, etchings, and photographs. Like the layers of civilization in *Topologie,* each distinct and yet topologically linked to other layers by common structures, actions, and desires, the works produced in collaboration and the texts taken from them and organized into the "spaces" of *Topologie* are quite disparate and yet maintain a complex series of linkages and echoes of each other.

The combination of text and image is particularly interesting because of the limitations each form imposes on the interpretation or reading of the other. The images of these artists do not lend themselves readily to a diegesis and yet there is always a diegetic level to Robbe-Grillet's novels. His procedure is to choose, in the Magritte paintings, for example, from among the many repetitions of elements, those which fit into his own personal arsenal of images. "Going through a retrospective exhibition of a painter whom he prefers to all others, the writer immediately picks out objects, stories. Figures come alive, the repetition of a theme becomes diachronic, the title of a painting surges forward like a pass word. . . ."[11] As these generative themes and images combine into a text, they move further and further away from the pictures that were their impulsion, while being at the same time reined in, limited to a certain extent by those same pictures and the need to include elements from them in the diegesis. Meaning circulates between image and text as they support each other, vectorize interpretation, and sometimes contradict each other.[12]

The choice of elements from the visual media to include in the text nevertheless remains Robbe-Grillet's. Thus, the first picture by Magritte shows a rock immobile above a view of the sea; on the rock is a castle. The first line in Part 5 of the "Cinquième Espace" in *Topologie* is, "It starts with a stone falling . . ." (128). The rock is no longer suspended but rather is falling and there is no mention whatsoever of the castle. But the falling rock has already appeared several times in *Topologie* and thus fits into the storehouse of possible themes to develop just as the image and the title of the picture *L'Assassin menacé* merges well with Robbe-Grillet's preoccupations dating all the way back to *Les Gommes*. Robbe-Grillet's task in the construction of *Topologie* was to find a way to combine the preoccupations he shared with Magritte with those he shared with Rauschenberg, Delvaux, and Hamilton and with those he had already explored in previous works. He does so here by allowing each major collaborative effort a separate space in which it may develop according to a topography he establishes and which is linked to all other spaces by a great number of common elements that penetrate through each of these spaces.

As the intertexual elements turn up in *Topologie,* they are subjected to manipulation and recombination according to another system of generation which Robbe-Grillet uses here for the first time systematically: generation based on letters in a word.[13] The seminal letter is certainly V, its form reproduced in the female crotch, in the V-shaped insignia stamped on a rock and on a ring, in the V-shaped slice out of a watermelon, in the closed V isosceles triangle of the top of the temples, in the prow of the ship, and in the volcano (its first letter and its shape). Each of these V-shaped objects implies the others as well; the juice from the slice of the watermelon suggests blood, the blood suggests the sacrifice perhaps of a young virgin in a temple and according to a ritual (signaled by the insignia in the rock). Other combinations are also made to link these elements, combinations which produce other narrative openings. The letter V generates the name Vanadé with its complex overdetermination *(surdétermination).* Vanadium, the ancient city dedicated to Vanadé, is also the name of a silver-white chemical (producing the proliferation of white objects, particularly in the all-white *cellule génératrice*) in group V of the periodic chart (producing the series of fives throughout *Topologie*) and whose atomic weight is around fifty.[14] A similar name, Vanadis, is one of the names given to the Norse goddess Freya, the goddess of love and beauty, and to her family, the gods of fertility (birth of the demigod David). One of the trans-

formations of Vanadé is Vanessa, the name of a butterfly; thus
butterflies appear in the text, overdetermined by their name and
their shape (two triangles).

Another transformation produces Diviana, thus *divin*—the
gods and Greek temples again—and *divan*—place of love and
of sacrificial offerings. Diviana becomes Diana and Diane, the
virgin goddess, who had a twin brother, here named David in
a further manipulation of the letters of Vanadé but also joining
the name David Hamilton. Like Vanessa, Diana is also a type
of butterfly and in alchemy refers to silver; like Vanadis, Diana
of Ephesus was a goddess of fertility whose famous statue is
covered with breasts. Diana was also called Diana Parthenos, the
maiden, suggesting the parthenogenic reproduction in the ancient
city Vanadium/Ephesus. Another transformation of Diana into
Danae is made in the text with the statement that Danae is not
Diana and should not be confused with her even though her
impregnation is also interesting. Danae was visited by Zeus in
her prison tower (joining the prison series, from the *cellule
génératrice* and the sequestered prostitutes and adolescent girls,
and the tower image from the Tarot cards and from the picture
of the tower in *Les Gommes*) in the form of a golden shower (joining
the butterfly images and producing the theft of golden coins
stamped with the image of Vanadé and scattered on the ground
in the fatal car accident mentioned in the text). As Vanadé generated white, Diana is the name of a color of blue, reinforcing
the azure of the sea and sky in *Topologie* and joining the color in
several of Magritte's paintings in *La Belle Captive*.[15]

In his textually exposed effort to teach his readers to read,
Robbe-Grillet gives a clear picture of exactly how this type of
lettristic manipulation can be productive and can generate narrative. Having established V as a generator, he introduces the
letter G on the banner of a ship. "This letter gives the following
series, which incidentally was only to be expected: vanadis—
vigil—vessel/danger—water's edge—diviner/plunge—in vain—
carnage/divan—virgin—vagina/gravid—engenders—david and
it is easy to see from the arrangement of the consonants that the
full name of this child would in fact be David G. Here is the

story" (37). The story announced is precisely that which would allow the integration of each of the words in the inscription in the order given. The story, the birth of David, which later becomes a play within the text directed or written by David H., takes place in Vanadium (Vanadis), where a young virgin standing guard (vigil) at the port sees a boat approaching (vessel). Sensing danger (danger) as the boat continues to approach the shore (water's edge), she consults an oracle (diviner) who advises the women to try to defend themselves in the water (plunge) rather than on land, where the superior physical strength of the males on the boat would surely defeat them. Although they do as instructed, it is to no avail (in vain) and they are all massacred (carnage) except the sentinel who had given the warning and who is captured by the soldiers. On a low sacrificial couch (divan), she is repeatedly raped (virgin, vagina). Her pubic area covered with blood, she runs into the sea, but she does not die and this is how David was born (gravid—engenders—david).[16] This story allows Robbe-Grillet a link with previous scenes and with scenes to come; the bloody screaming girl running from the temple described in the second section is the violated virgin, and later the *Birth of David,* the play, becomes a reenactment centuries later of the same story.

Although the manipulation of letters as a generative device functioned in his previous works, Robbe-Grillet has always been more interested in the referent of the entire word as his generator and not merely in a single letter or group of letters. The lettristic games of *Topologie* are an experiment for Robbe-Grillet about which he is not particularly enthusiastic: ". . . having completed this text, it no longer amuses me. Having done it once used up all its appeal."[17] Robbe-Grillet sees this technique as a dead-end because it has, in a sense, already been legitimized by the theory that explains it. If a theory is able to account for a work before the work itself exists, the work itself becomes superfluous. Although Robbe-Grillet expects, and even desires, eventual recuperation of his work by critics and theorists, it is unlikely that he will again use extensive lettristic manipulations which he had once found so fascinating in the work of Raymond Roussel.

Development

As the narrative line becomes increasingly diffuse with *Topologie,* the movement of the narration becomes more complex. Recalling the technique of reverse nomination used particularly in *Dans le labyrinthe* and in *Projet pour une révolution à New York,* the *cellule génératrice* begins as a cubical white room with a window. On closer inspection the narrator sees that the window has bars. But bars on the window suggest that the place is a prison; thus, existence preceding essence, the cubical room becomes a prison. This kind of increasingly closer inspection, movement toward a construction, often followed by penetration and definition of the structure, regulates a number of the descriptions in *Topologie.* "Formerly commanding the entire system, a building constructed in wrought iron . . . occupies the rear of the scene. . . . The building has extensive cellars, as witness the row of small oblong windows running the whole length of the facade at ground level. . . . Moreover some of the underground rooms are even completely without ventilation from the outside, as, for example, the storeroom in which bottles of wine, neatly arranged in rows one on top of another, appear. . . . It is here amid the litter of glass and dusty cobwebs that the last murder was committed . . ." (120). This movement into the structures is emphasized in the many expressions like "seen from closer up," "on approaching one sees that," "looking more closely," etc., but in this example and in many others progression toward a goal is accomplished in the swell of the description itself, which begins with the overall structure of the building, the next sentence taking up the building again but this time moving toward the base of the structure and the row of windows which lead into subterranean rooms in which the murder was committed. Overlapping the end of one idea and the beginning of the next is a narrative echo of the small waves on the surface of the water in the port of Vanadium. A similar operation links paragraphs.

In the section entitled "Cérémonie rituelle," a paragraph ends with "She drinks" (113). The next paragraph takes up the "She drinks," moves on to other things, and ends with "she listens," which in turn becomes the first words of the following paragraph, each paragraph connected to the last by a duplication, as in a game of dominoes, an open circuitry in which one description leads to the next, which leads to the next, and so on.

One particular problem Robbe-Grillet faced in *Topologie* was how to move from one "Espace" to the next. The most interesting solution appears between the "Premier Espace" and the "Deuxième Espace." The "Premier Espace" ends: "But he has to wait until everything is motionless again, the cycle as a whole having been closed by a specious, nonrecurring, descending movement in the generative cell" (53). This last sentence and the title of the next act as a fulcrum between the two spaces. "Ascending rehearsals for a motionless dwelling" (55) reverses the elements of the last sentence of the "Premier Espace" as the artist's etchings reverse the reality of the model before her in a point/counterpoint. The word "rehearsals," i.e., repetitions in the "Deuxième Espace," comes from "nonrecurring," at the end of the "Premier Espace," itself contradicted by "cycle" and "again"; "ascending" reverses "descending"; "dwelling" grows out of "cell"; and the final "motionless" completes the symmetry, challenging "movement." The ascending movement, which grows out of its counterpoint of the previous section (Mrs. Hamilton and her twins going down the tower), is David Hamilton walking upstairs.

Finally, since construction is the primary preoccupation in *Topologie,* it is not surprising to find also many examples of reverse construction, examples of deconstruction. Each of the five sections of the Incipit, introduced by the narrator affirming his own consciousness ("Before I fall asleep"), is deconstructed one after the other by the repeated denial of the narrative just before: "But there is nothing left." At the same time as the description constructs, it seeks to take itself down again point by point. The same type of affirmation/denial occurs in the daydreams of one of the young girls in the old house; after each of her reveries, she pouts: "No! That's all wrong" (91). Less obviously but with the same effect in "Premier Espace" in particular, a number of paragraphs begin with "on the contrary," "however," "nevertheless," "unfortunately," "but," all signaling information in contradiction to what the reader is thought to assume. The plan for this technique is explained on the piece of washed-out paper the narrator fishes from the river: "(1) analysis of the probable meaning of the maxim, (2) it is quite true, (3) it is totally false, (4) conclusion suggesting other possible meanings" (78). But the warning that the text would be slippery comes at the very beginning: ". . . I write the word CONSTRUCTION, an illusionist painting, a make-believe constructon by which I name the ruins of a future deity" (11). This is an imaginary construction, an optical illusion, the ruins of a building that never existed.

The source of the narration becomes increasingly diffuse in *Topologie*. Although the narrators of *La Maison de rendez-vous* and *Projet pour une révolution à New York* shifted, the narrative voice here can never be attached to any specific character. In fact there are no actual characters in *Topologie* despite the series of names attached to figures who appear briefly and then disappear. At best there are groups into which these figures can be organized: the girls in the prison cell, the girls in the old house, the sacrifice victims, the male figures. The blurred consciousness of the narrator from the Incipit returns as the ambiguous murderer/detective in "Le Criminel déjà sur mes propres traces" [The Criminal Already on My Own Trail]. He is again in a fog and unsure: "It's morning. It's evening. I remember" (107). It is ultimately this ambiguous and hesitant narrator who is "laboriously reconstructing the plan day after day, through repetitions, contradictions, and omissions" (138) that constitute the book.

Chapter Nine
Souvenirs du triangle d'or

Like *Topologie d'une cité fantôme, Souvenirs du triangle d'or* (1978) is made up of texts published elsewhere and structured on the imaginative linkages possible between these blocks of text.[1] Like the Surrealist's hope that the juxtaposition of ordinary, unrelated objects within the same creative space would trigger an insight into the mysterious and marvelous linkages among all physical objects, the juxtapositioning of texts which have certain specific functions in their original contexts forces new narrative patterns to emerge from them. The texts Robbe-Grillet combines in *Souvenirs,* as in one of the collages of scraps of newspaper which he has done, all come from collaborations with other artists—Magritte again, Jasper Johns, and the photographer Irina Ionesco (not related to Ionesco, the playwright/author)—and are preceded, succeeded, and linked together by new narrative passages.[2] After a preparation of about thirty pages of new text, the next fifty pages of *Souvenirs* repeat the second, third, and fourth parts of *La Belle Captive,* a collection of seventy-seven paintings by René Magritte accompanied by a text by Robbe-Grillet (the first part of *La Belle Captive* had already been published in *Topologie d'une cité fantôme*). The next previously unpublished eight pages lead into an eighteen-page text published with photos by Irina Ionesco in *Temple aux miroirs.* These pictures are for the most part taken in luxurious, stylized settings with half-nude women and very young girls in erotic poses.[3] Another fifteen pages of new text lead to another text, published separately as *La Cible,* the twenty-page preface to the catalog for an art exhibit by Jasper Johns which had taken place at the Centre Pompidou in Paris in 1978. The last section of the book is eighty-seven pages of previously unpublished material and provides the space for the

131

rich, complex relationships among the block of texts to resolve themselves.

Each of these blocks of text has thematic unity within itself and each one proposes pieces of a different story line and a different direction toward which meaning may develop. All these possible directions for meaning are meant to be retained in the reader's mind in spite of the contradictions among them. The hallways described at one time as being part of a large house with many rooms, recalling the hallways in *Topologie d'une cité fantôme* through which the David Hamilton character walked, later become hallways in a prison joining the many prison cells, and at another point, almost losing their spatial qualities, become the links between strange scenes which seem to be enacted by imprisoned young women. But these hallways are never only one or another of these possible descriptions; they are all of them at the same time. Robbe-Grillet's fascination with this variety of meaning lies in the possibility of shifting from one interpretation to another. Thus, the author's task in writing a collage/text consists of developing a logistics for getting from one interpretation to another without valorizing one of them over the others. By the same token larger segments of text, narrative segments, exist simultaneously, contradicting each other, borrowing from each other, and transforming fragments of meaning (i.e., objects, gestures, characters, situations, forms) to fit into different contexts, in which these fragments function differently and must be interpreted differently. None of these narrative segments is basic, and yet, as Robbe-Grillet says, his purpose in including and combining them in a single novel is not to create a text in which there are several interpenetrating plots which, like Balzac's *Comédie humaine,* together form a complex but single meaningful whole.[4] Rather the contradictions and interpenetrations of events and narrative elements are the explorations of the multiplicity of meaning.

In his study of the sources of *Souvenirs* Bruce Morrissette wonders whether a reader not familiar with *La Belle Captive* in particular would be able to understand what is meant in the section of *Souvenirs* which is a repetition of the last three sections of *La*

Belle Captive. How could a reader interpret, for example, the mention of a falling rock in *Souvenirs* if he were not aware that this falling rock is the first of Magritte's paintings selected by Robbe-Grillet for *La Belle Captive* and that similar rocks recur in other Magritte paintings? Similarly one might wonder if the many references to previous works, so easily recognizable to some-one familiar with Robbe-Grillet's work, put at a great disadvan-tage the reader whose first contact with Robbe-Grillet is, for example, *Souvenirs*. Yet Robbe-Grillet's novels are not meant to be private jokes or puzzles for the initiated. In fact one of the most important, for Robbe-Grillet, and intriguing aspects of a book like *Souvenirs* is the new story that a previously appearing text becomes when placed next to different narrative segments. The meanings of the texts in *La Belle Captive,* texts which are interpreted by the pictures and whose meanings have a tendency to ossify when placed beside a picture, are challenged and are forced to shift, to communicate something new. More so than ever before, in *Souvenirs* Robbe-Grillet's real concern in writing becomes apparent: to use form to challenge meaning when mean-ing begins to install itself as truth and to use meaning to challenge form when form begins to become its own justification for ex-isting. The uninitiated reader of Robbe-Grillet is not necessarily at a disadvantage; on the contrary, he may have the advantage of being free from previously developed meanings. Rather than recognizing the image of the falling rock as a reference to Ma-gritte, such an untainted reader would attempt to forge new connections between this rock and other elements of the text he reads. In fact so great is the influence of visual stimulus that the reader who has once seen the Magritte paintings in *La Belle Captive,* the Delvaux paintings in *Construction d'un temple en ruines à la déesse Vanadé,* the Ionesco photos in *Temple aux miroirs,* the Rauschenberg lithographs in *Traces suspectes en surface,* and the Johns paintings with *La Cible* can never again read the Robbe-Grillet texts accompanying these art works without visualizing the paintings or photos, a situation which at once enriches and impoverishes the reading of the written text by adding the images of the art works into the interpretation but at the same time tending to limit the interpretation of the text to the possibilities suggested by those images.

Souvenirs du triangle d'or begins with a few introductory paragraphs which recall the Incipit of *Topologie d'une cité fantôme.* The narrating voice, complaining that everything is shrinking, describes "the general plan," which will be modified but "without changing—it is too late—anything about the elements which make it up, henceforth inevitable" (7), these unchangeable constituent parts being the blocks of previously published material knitted together in *Souvenirs* into a total pattern. As "things" seem to shrink together enclosing the narrator in this unsituated space neither clearly inside nor outside but in front of a door with no door knob or door bell and which cannot be opened, "This is where the story begins, after a probable interruption, quite distinct [the first of the blank spaces to appear on the printed pages separating sections of the narrative], giving the impression that things are still shrinking: just the opposite of an opening. The totality of the system remains, for the moment, rigorously immobile" (9). The "totality of the system" will be the creation of the links necessary to join disparate texts, an entrapment and a fixation of meaning toward a direction determined by the orientations of the other texts.

But somehow movement must begin, and after a blank space on the page, a tiny, fragile, transitory whisper barely perceptible allows the narrative to come into focus and to begin to create an ever-broadening framework in which the incidents of this novel become possible. As the center of focus broadens from this minute original movement, it encompasses first only grains of sand disturbed by this suggestion of a whisper, then includes the wave pattern formed by the sand on planks of wood making up an abandoned terrace near the sea. If this scene is perceptible, a consciousness must be registering it, and a first-person narrator appears. The events of the story begin as this narrator introduces a variety of new characters: a girl on horseback pursued by hunters, a beggar-prostitute dragging a fur behind her, and finally two policemen who confront the narrator with a newspaper picture of a young woman who has apparently been tortured and killed.

In the now-familiar Robbe-Grillet manner this newspaper picture comes alive and the narrator enters the picture mentally, in imagination or in memory, and wonders if he himself is the girl's murderer. The picture freezes again and the action returns to the terrace where the narrator is arrested by the two policemen.

After a blank interval a first-person narrator, perhaps the man who has just been arrested, perhaps not, describes a newspaper report of a murder investigation. Walking along a half-destroyed part of town, police inspector Franck V. Francis finds a woman's bloodstained blue high-heeled shoe in the street in front of a suspicious door with no bell or knob. But Franck V. Francis implicates himself in the murder of a young woman and soldiers arrive at his door. After another blank space on the page, the next three sections are reprints of the second, third, and fourth sections of *La Belle Captive*. A first-person narrator in a prison cell resumes, describing the sights and sounds he registers in his cell. He imagines himself at another time when he was an elegantly dressed doctor and the scene changes back to the terraced beachside restaurant where the first-person narrator sits watching young girls play ball in the sand. He notices a young woman who seems to be a student sitting at another table, tricks her into smoking a drugged cigarette, and, with the help of passers-by who believe him to be a physician, loads the unconscious girl into his car. But the girl, aware of the plot against her, has only pretended to be drugged and, when the false doctor least expects it, pulls a hypodermic needle out of her boot and injects him with a drug.

After another pause a first-person narrator undergoes an interrogation in which he must explain the presence of certain objects in his account. He describes strange rituals requiring virgin girls as sacrificial offerings and complains of always having to repeat the same old stories haunted by the same old obsessions. After a pause the first-person narrator begins again. He had just awakened and he takes up a monologue which moves him quickly around in time and space from the beach to the Opera House, to a casino, to a prison cell, and finally to a place where he holds prisoner a beautiful young woman.

The next short section is a transition between *La Belle Captive* and the text from *Temple aux miroirs.* The first-person narrator leaves his house for the theater, where he meets Vanessa, a student, who tells him the story of the death of King Boris at the hands of revolutionary insurgents.[5] Her story merges with the play being performed. The narrator leaves the theater and runs into Temple, a flower girl, who gives him a false apple in which is hidden an electronic device which opens the door to a sanctuary; this door has no knob or bell. Once the narrator is inside the sanctuary the text resumes as a reprint of *Temple aux miroirs.* The narrator walks down an ever-turning hallway and is confronted with a series of strange scenes involving beautiful women prisoners, some nude, some strapped into chairs with strings of pearls. Temple reappears in this strange place and like Alice walks through mirrors into different scenes.

In the transition between *Temple aux miroirs* and *La Cible,* the text written for Jasper Johns, the first-person narrator returns to the prison cell, seemingly having been accused of some crime by a Lady G. In the cell a disembodied hand appears through a grilled opening and drops objects on the floor. The hand drops a lightbulb which breaks on the floor, forming a target consisting of nine circles. For each circle the narrator finds an object which has already appeared in the text or will appear and whose shape is similar to the numbers nine through one. When the narrator completes the series, the hand gives him a flashlight and leaves the cell door open. After stumbling around in the darkness, presumably outside his cell, the narrator realizes he has actually never left the cell.

All the material from this point in the text to the end is new, bringing in themes already explored in the text, like the theme of the sphere—pearls, balls, lightbulbs, a bald head—and themes not directly described before in *Souvenirs* but which appear in or are very close to scenes in other works: a girl chased through a forest by dogs; a girl's body served to be eaten; a girl in a coffin surrounded by lit candles; a girl being nailed to a cross in some kind of erotic ritual. The last section of *Souvenirs* is an account, half accurate, half newly invented, of the incidents described in the book, and some not described but which could have occurred, given in twelve-minute intervals from 7:00 A.M. to 3:36 P.M. In a final paragraph a first-person narrator wonders what he has accomplished.

Contamination of Meaning

If we believe, as Robbe-Grillet encourages us to, that his main concern in writing is to follow and to control the interplay between the natural tendency to create meaning and the systematic disruption of meaning made possible by an attention to form and not to meaning, it is not difficult to explain the recurrence of the same themes throughout Robbe-Grillet's work. He allows himself the indulgence of describing and playing with sado-erotic desires and images that haunt him. Since structuring the components of a work is more important than the components themselves, Robbe-Grillet chooses components that haunt him or that haunt his world or culture partly in order that they may lose their ability to haunt by having been placed within a structure that robs them of their impact. In addition, all structuring involves repetition, the repetition that establishes a pattern, and the repeated use of already explored themes necessarily highlights the structures rather than the elements which go into the formation of the structures. Control of the components thus is greater; the danger of slipping into meaningfulness decreases.

If Robbe-Grillet is concerned that his novels not become "meaningful," that is, that they not express truths, his characters often have the opposite approach. As any good detective would, Franck V. Francis and other narrators frequently wonder about and seek the cause for certain effects they notice, the meaning of certain events, the answers to their questions, the logic behind certain behaviors. But the thrust of the whole text is systematically to undermine the logic of the real world and replace it with the logic of the text. Again as in *Les Gommes* and in *Topologie d'une cité fantôme* the detective discovers himself to have been the criminal. The narrators of this text therefore repeatedly express their fear of traps, errors, or contradictions that might lead to an impasse in the text. When such impasses occur the narrator is forced to begin at some other point in his story; certain kinds of impasses force the narrator back into his cell, and he must discover new ways to describe his situation so that he can again be transported into other times and places.

Robbe-Grillet suggests that there are several ways in which the events of this book can be put together to form a variety of stories, each with its own narrator, who himself plays a part in the stories of the other narrators even though none of the stories coincides on the surface. One of the stories is that of a man in prison who is periodically interrogated and probably given consciousness-altering drugs to make him reveal his crime, which probably involved sex and which he tries to avoid revealing by describing his cell. Another is that of a doctor who also uses drugs to get young girls to relate sexual fantasies. There is also the story of a man impersonating a policeman in order to cover up his own crimes. And there are various subplot adventures common to several of the stories, including drug smuggling; the operations of a secret society which abducts virgin women, tortures, and kills them in fulfillment of rituals; and the revolts and acts of vandalism of a gang of adolescents. Many elements of these diverse narrational centerpoints overlap and have a different significance depending upon which story they appear in at any given moment. Since they overlap, the development of one plot may abruptly veer off into another through the intermediary of a common element. These shifts to another track often occur through the many narrators. The narrator in his prison cell reflects upon his physical appearance, the black stubble that covers his head and chin, and his present resemblance to pictures of assassins that used to make him laugh when he was an elegant gentleman. The well-dressed gentleman referred to, who looks like a doctor and therefore impersonates a doctor, takes over the narrative, and another story begins in which the doctor describes his abduction of a young student.

But such shifts in narrative point of view can also have an impact on the surface events or on the reader's assumptions based on the events. Franck V. Francis's pursuit of his fruitless investigation of the possible connection between the bloodstained shoe

he has found and the murder of a young woman began as the
account of a first-person narrator of a newspaper article. In the
course of the newspaper account the third-person narration of
Franck V. Francis's investigation suddenly switches to first person. This first person makes a statement that would seem to
incriminate him: he wonders whether his colleague suspects him
of anything. The character of Franck V. Francis, an innocent and
naive police inspector, now overlaps with that of this first-person
narrator, who appears to be guilty of something; their stories
occupy the same textual space. As a result, Franck's possession
of the shoe is no longer innocent; rather it becomes evidence to
connect him to murder. The text returns to third-person narration
after only a few lines, but it is too late; Franck V. Francis has
been incriminated. The heretofore entirely dutiful police inves-
tigator suddenly begins to worry about whether he has made
mistakes that might lead to his downfall. And in fact he has. He
allowed a guilty first person to take over his narration, writing
suspect statements into his text.

The next scene takes place in a prison cell. Who actually
occupies that cell is never clear. "The man is alone, in the silence,
in the middle of the cell. And little by little, as if cautiously,
I realize that it is I, probably" (41). Even the first-person narrator
is not sure whether or not he is the one in the cell; he cannot be
sure because all the characters overlap and merge. They share a
common history, physiognomy, and fate, even if these normally
stable parameters of the individual are variable here. The individuals referred to in the text as Franck V. Francis, Dr. Morgan,
Inspector Duchamp, he, or I are like fragments of the same
schizophrenic personality and recall another privileged image of
Robbe-Grillet's, that of bits of disparate junk floating in a body
of water. Each bit of junk is a fragment of some potential history of existence and each bit, carrying with it the memory or trace
of that other existence, combines with other bits, each of these
also carrying its load of narrative, to form new combinations
varying continuously with the seemingly random and yet systematic movement of the waves.

For this reason it is never entirely clear whether any given first-person narrator is the same first-person narrator as in another part of the text. When the first-person narrator in his prison cell has a hard time distinguishing himself from a caricature of a villainous criminal in the newspaper and from the elegantly dressed doctor on the terrace of the café, the difficulty arises from the fact that he shares with them the same textual body. Thus, this character in the prison is contiguous with the elegant false doctor on the terrace because the doctor is the narrator's memory of himself. Since he also resembles the criminal in the newspaper photo, the doctor does so as well. The self simply cannot be defined or limited to I or he.

The same kind of fluidity of boundaries between individual characters exists among the females, but female voices take up the narrative much less frequently. Under the influence of Dr. Morgan's drugs, Angelica remembers incidents from her past in which her name is Christine, which is also the name of Lady G (who appeared in *Topologie d'une cité fantôme* and who recalls Lady Ava in *La Maison de rendez-vous*) as a child. Lady G is also called Caroline née de Saxe, the name of one of the girls in Robbe-Grillet's film *Le Jeu avec le feu*, and her story becomes overlapped with that of Nathalie, who appears in the same film. At the same time Angelica shares characteristics of the young student/secret agent and her interrogation recalls that of the little girl, Laura, in *Projet pour une révolution à New York*.

Linking Texts

That little girl at the same time recalls Temple in *Souvenirs*, a character with greater stability than any of the other female or male characters. Unlike the other female figures Temple is never a victim, and she never takes up the narration in *Souvenirs*. Her role seems to be primarily one of linkage between the text of *La Belle Captive* and *La Cible*, in which no little girl has a role, to *Temple aux miroirs*, in which the little girl is quite important. Temple is the rose vendor on the bridge, recalling and thereby bringing into play from *La Belle Captive* Magritte's painting of a man walking across a bridge and seemingly accompanied by

a girl-sized rose, *La Boîte de Pandore.* In *Souvenirs* Temple is the
one who holds the key to the sanctuary, the green apple. This
apple figures in *La Belle Captive* in Magritte's *La Chambre d'écoute,*
where a huge apple fills an entire room, and in *La Grande Guerre,*
where a perfect and perfectly symmetrical shiny green apple ob-
scures or perhaps replaces the features of a man's face. The sanctuary to which Temple's apple allows access is a space whose
definition shifts, like the defining features of the characters in
Souvenirs, from prison to theater to hideout for captured young
women.

In the sanctuary of *Temple aux miroirs* are other elements which
serve as connectors among the texts joined in *Souvenirs,* the blue
high-heeled shoe, the mirrors (which reappear on the shoe as well
as in the prison cell and in a beach cabana), and the sphere images
in various forms. Pearls drop onto and rebound from a mirror
and produce a sound like the drops of water into a puddle deep
in an underground cave or dungeon, a sound which the prisoner
in *La Cible* hears later. These pearls also encircle the young female
prisoners' wrists, strapping them into chairs, and their necks,
like dog collars. The pearls around the neck used as restraints
prepare for the later images of dogs hunting down a girl running
through the forest. The narrator's head is also described as round
and hairless like the lightbulb which is dropped into the prisoner's
cell or like the beachball which appears throughout the book and
is connected to sexual arousal, exhibitionism, and voyeurism in
the scenes in which bikini-clad young women play ball under the
gaze of a man on the terrace.

The theme of the ball comes to a paroxysm during an interrogation of a female prisoner/narrator. Twice her description of
her prison cell begins to move toward the outside in a description
of the exits, the hallways, the door, and the window, leading to
the outside and to freedom. Each time her description is cut short
by the imperious, omniscient, and impersonal controller of the
interrogation. The prisoner tries another escape technique and
begins to describe the sound and image of a ball bouncing around
in the cubical cell, a ball which undergoes transformation in
succeeding lines to a bubble, a pearl, a beachball, the frothy

bubbles of foam on the sea, a tennis ball, a Ping-Pong ball, a lightbulb, the bald head of the narrator, a crystal ball, a Christmas tree ornament. The effect of the rebounding ball becomes hypnotic; the narrator loses words (". . . the height changes no doubt imperceptibly at each of its . . . (of its what?) . . ." [158]) or becomes stuck on certain words (". . . without, however, confirming that impression in any definite way, even after a period of time quite . . . of time quite . . . of time quite . . ." [158]). Finally the image of the ball bouncing around the cell provides the desired escape vehicle, becomes the interstices between two textual spaces. "Once again I try—but in vain—to follow with my eyes the luminous sphere in its ceaseless trajectory" (158). Because this statement recalls the description of the beachball, it blurs the frame of the previous lines. "And now, once again, it [or she] is in a large forest with rectilinear, vertical trunks, so high that their tops get lost towards the invisible sky" (158). The pronoun "it" (*elle* in French, which could refer to the sphere or the girl) is the transit point between the cell and the outside, referring to the "luminous sphere" in the previous sentence and to Nathalie in the following sentence. The sphere is thus associated with the female and seemingly with a means to freedom whereas previously the sphere (the pearls) had served to bind the female prisoners in the "temple."

The need to find elements common to each of the blocks of previously written texts or to transform elements in those texts in such a way that they could be diegetically linked to other texts has resulted in a book in which the adventures and ultimate fate of various thematic objects are extremely complex. Rather than following the fate of a person, the reader is asked to follow the ups and downs in the ability of various objects to display links to other objects in order to create a story strictly through their physical characteristics. For aside from any general philosophical or psychological conclusions one might draw from the repeated inclusion of certain objects, the relationships established among the objects are characterized by surface features, and the meanings these relationships suggest are always diegetic, superficial. Oddly enough many years after the publication of *Les Gommes,* Barthes's

"Littérature objective," *Pour un Nouveau Roman,* and Robbe-Grillet's subsequent rejection of the object and of description of the
physical features of the object for its own sake as ultimately
uninteresting, in *Souvenirs* there is a return to objects, to the
physical features of objects, but a return guided by some fifteen
years of literary experimentation. Thus, *Souvenirs* resembles very
little *Les Gommes,* but it does provide the kind of text for which
Robbe-Grillet had been criticized in the early 1950s and which
he had not in fact written, a text where the real adventure is that
of the nonhuman elements of the text and the nonhumanistic
elements of the characters, their forms and functions.

It is easy to see why Robbe-Grillet is so interested in the visual
arts. The printers and photographers with whom Robbe-Grillet
collaborates have provided him with the raw material for his
work, raw material which is not only rich and varied in itself but
which has the additional advantage of reflecting the fantasies and
obsessions of other human beings. Some of these fantasies or
obsessions clearly coincide with those of Robbe-Grillet.[6] The
desire for this raw material explains why the work Robbe-Grillet
did with Delvaux was less satisfying to him than his work with
the paintings by Magritte. Delvaux essentially illustrated Robbe-
Grillet's text, thereby robbing Robbe-Grillet of the change in
orientation that the input of Delvaux's own unique interests or
obsessions might have added. Robbe-Grillet was confronted not
with new material from Delvaux but rather with more Robbe-
Grillet material dressed in Delvaux characteristics. With
Magritte, on the other hand, and by the same token with Rauschenberg, Johns, and Ionesco, Robbe-Grillet was forced to deal
with and to shape to his own ends the already-formulated obsessions of another artist. Morrissette finds disappointing the fact
that the Robbe-Grillet text that accompanies *Temple aux miroirs*
seems to be merely a rather faithful description of the photos.
The richness of the implications, the structural implications, of
this text becomes apparent, however, in *Souvenirs* as Robbe-Grillet
is forced to account for descriptions which had had as template
the obsessions of another. The rich variety this infusion from
other creative minds offers Robbe-Grillet can be seen in increased

numbers of desultory items now floating in his canal: beer cans, a ruler, apples and oranges, a whole zoo of animals, a jewel on a shoe (the shoe itself a familiar Robbe-Grillet fetish), pearls, a flashlight. Each of these items can set off a narrative chain, and, in combination, they automatically produce a story. The notion of the omniscient, godlike author creating life was replaced in the 1950s and 1960s by Barthes's and Ricardou's image of the writer as *scripteur* and explorer of structures and forms. The story writer who had disappeared during this time is now perhaps returning, but as a story writer enriched by his awareness of the potential contributions that can be made to the story when the writer allows the development of the story to be dictated at least in part by the shapes, semantic resonances, and intertextual associations of the very elements that go to make up the story.

Chapter Ten
Un Régicide

Robbe-Grillet rightly considers his long unpublished first novel *Un Régicide* (1978) more advanced than *Les Gommes* and perhaps even than *Le Voyeur* and *La Jalousie;* he finds it more disturbing, a more radical departure from traditional narrative form than the three subsequent novels even though he made no substantial revisions of the original 1949 text. Its oneiric and rather lyrical tone also sets it apart from the rest of his works.[1] Furthermore, this early work makes obvious references to Robbe-Grillet's life. The opening sequences of the book describe a recurrent dream of Robbe-Grillet's and the entire island setting was inspired by his experiences and memories of living on the Breton coast. Perhaps the most surprising feature of this text, finally published in the same year as *Souvenirs du triangle d'or,* is the large number of elements in *Un Régicide* which were to resurface in Robbe-Grillet's later novels. The constancy of the appearance of these themes throughout his career as a novelist lends credence to Robbe-Grillet's admission in "Fragment autobiographique imaginaire" that he has never written about anything but himself, his fantasies and obsessions, even in novels which may have seemed to readers at the time to be devoid of human emotion. The weight of evidence argues for a Robbe-Grillet giving vent to his personal phantoms; but only the perspective afforded by the availability of the entire corpus of works allows these patterns to emerge.

Un Régicide was written during 1948 and 1949. Robbe-Grillet sent the manuscript to Gallimard, but it was rejected, according to Robbe-Grillet, because the editors felt that although it was an interesting piece, this type of novel did not correspond to the expectations of readers and therefore would not sell.[2] After the publication of *Les Gommes,* Robbe-Grillet considered reworking his *Régicide* manuscript but soon abandoned it in favor of a new book he was working on, *Le Voyeur.* Once again in 1957 he began to revise the text but soon found that his revisions were so extensive that he was simply writing another book entirely, and he again put aside *Un Régicide.* Finally in 1978 Robbe-Grillet decided simply to publish the manuscript more or less in its original version. The only major change, made in the 1957 revisions, was the name of the main character from Philippe to Boris, a name which appears in nearly all the novels and films, thus creating intertextual linkage. (Robbe-Grillet also feels Boris is a more neutral name, emptier of meanings or connotations.) In addition there are other minor changes made in 1957, mainly in the first ten pages, that were retained in the published text.

When Robbe-Grillet talks about the impact that his own real life has on his literature, he describes the process as indirect. His experiences are stored away in his memory and his subconscious mind goes to work on these memories, transforming and recombining them even before they undergo the reformation necessary to be included in a piece of art. Since *Un Régicide* was Robbe-Grillet's first novel, written when he was in his late twenties, this transformational process had not yet had either much time to accomplish the kinds of changes Robbe-Grillet speaks of or much material to transform. Therefore, *Un Régicide* is the most personal and most autobiographical of Robbe-Grillet's novels. The drab, foggy island is an image of the coast of Brittany, where Robbe-Grillet spent his summers as a boy; the opening sequence is a recurrent dream; the factory in which Boris works is the one in which Robbe-Grillet himself worked during his war years in Nuremberg.

Unlike the subjects treated in any of his other books, political issues play a role in the diegesis; in all the other works Robbe-Grillet's political positions emerge only metaphorically as his novels challenge the authority of a ruling literary ideology and by extension any ruling political system. The politics of *Un Régicide* seem to reflect disenchantment with political systems since, as Robbe-Grillet points out nearly thirty years after the

novel was written,[3] it is not possible to determine whether the
Church party of the novel is extreme right or extreme left, only
that any democratic system has completely broken down; the
people are manipulated by the state to such an extent that even
their fantasy escapes from the real world are perhaps provided by
the government. The disillusionment with political systems reflected in this novel stems perhaps not only from a predictable
distaste for right-wing authoritarian governments just a few years
after the war with Nazi Germany but also from Robbe-Grillet's
unhappy trip to Communist Bulgaria as well as disappointment
in the democratic regimes of Western Europe at a time in which
the increasing alienation of individuals from their society was
reflected in the growth of absurdist literature and public respon-
siveness to characters like Camus's Meursault in *L'Etranger.*

In an interview in 1959 Robbe-Grillet says somewhat tongue
in cheek that his purpose in writing *Un Régicide* was to describe
fog.[4] Later in 1978, however, he says that *Un Régicide* is an
attempt to describe a schizoid life lived on two planes at the same
time. The fourteen chapters of the novel move along two levels,
describing real events in the life of Boris, the young protagonist,
and his fantasy life (his or that of an alter ego) on a desolate island
perhaps off the Breton coast whose permanent, isolated population
is only men. These two planes of existence occasionally make
contact, but for the most part remain separate. The "real" life
is written as third-person narrative from Boris's point of view;
the life on the island is described in first-person narration. The
novel opens with the description of a dream. The first-person
narrator is walking along a beach at dusk and must cross a treach-
erous stretch of coast between rocks and pits into which the waves
of the ocean rush, producing whirlpools which could drag the
hapless narrator out into the sea. The fading daylight makes his
chore all the more difficult, but he manages to reach a stretch
of flat sand just in time. The narrative changes to third person
with a description of Boris getting up on a Sunday morning in
August. He is to meet his friend Laura, a political activist, at
a café. As he waits for her, the narration slips back, as if it were
Boris's daydream, to the island again, which the first-person

narrator describes as isolated, dreary, and with a suffocatingly unchanging climate. The brown and gray landscape is always shrouded in fog; no outsider ever visits the island.

The next day Boris goes to his job at a factory where he works calculating productivity, but again Boris seems to slip into a daydream in which the first-person narrator, walking along the familiar paths of his native island, spots a stranger. At the factory at lunch time and in the train on the way home from work Boris hears conversations about the political situation in the country where the Church party has just won a majority in the government. Conversation also centers around the reported murder of a foreign student whose body was found on a deserted construction site which Boris first says he did and then did not visit the day before. Abruptly he is described walking among the scaffolds and pathways of the construction area where he comes upon a tombstone inscribed "Here lies Red," the name of the murdered student. An anagrammatical recombination of the letters in the French phrase "Ci-git Red" produces the word "Régicide." Back in town Laura comes to see Boris and to encourage him to work to gain the people's emotional support for the Church party now that there will be no more elections. She tells him that the kindly, popular figurehead monarch will be maintained and will serve as a unifying symbol of the country for the Church party. As she talks Boris's mind wanders and mentally he tries to persuade Laura to follow him into his daydream of walking along a calm beach into the warm ocean at night, following the song of the sirens. He pays no attention to her concerns about the future of the Church party and she leaves. The next day Boris is eager to read anything he can find about the activities of the king. He decides that in order to become truly close to the king, to play a unique role in his life, he will assassinate him, and he is suddenly filled with a sense of well-being.

On the island the first-person narrator walks toward the lighthouse tower in which lives, perhaps, the stranger whom he had seen earlier. His dread of the tower dissipates as he climbs up to the top of its crenellated walls; he notices that the long-awaited spring is beginning. He soon becomes friendly with the solitary keeper of the lighthouse tower, Malus, who tells him of the coming of the sirens.

In town Boris learns that the king will be coming in September to visit the factory. On the way home from work he buys a poster of the king, hangs it on the wall of his room, and begins to devise a plan to assassinate him. He will wait for the king on the abandoned second floor of the factory; as the king rides the one-man, open elevator past this landing, Boris will stop the elevator and stab the king.

On the island the first-person narrator is anticipating the joy of the coming of the sirens when the island's perennial clouds will disappear and the puny, dull, barely noticeable flowers of the sunless island will be replaced by real flowers blooming in vivid colors. The narrator walks along the beach with his siren, Aimone, but Malus is anxious and warns the narrator not to return to the sirens the next day. To the sorrow of the narrator Malus stops appearing on the island and the weather again turns gray and damp.

On the day the king is to visit the factory, Boris awaits him on the second-floor landing; but time goes by so slowly that distracting images are superimposed on Boris's purpose, images of himself standing alone on the beach watching Aimone swim away into the ocean. Suddenly the elevator begins to move and the smiling king appears in front of Boris, who stabs him and, covered with blood, runs down the stairs and through the crowd. That night he sleeps deeply and long. The next day he tears up the king's picture, but then he hears the king's voice coming from the neighbor's radio; the picture reappears whole on the wall. Boris has his bloody knife to prove his assassination attempt but now the bloodstains look like simple rust, and he cleans the knife.

On the island because of the days of warm sun, the plants have grown so fast and wildly that the inhabitants can no longer find their way around the most familiar places. But the sirens have left and the rain and fog have returned so dense and invasive that men have walked into the sea and have drowned without realizing that they were in water, thinking they were still breathing the thick wet air.

In town Boris is arrested by two policemen, who make him carry the sack with the king's dead body in it. But because of the weight of his load, he falls so far behind the policemen that he loses sight of them, throws the sack into an abandoned construction site, and goes to work. There he finds that he has been assumed dead and replaced at his job by the very efficient Red. Boris tries to prove to his coworkers that he has killed the king and shows them the sack with the king's body but they say this is insufficient proof.

On the island the fog becomes thicker still and people's houses and furniture begin to shrink. The men sit around telling stories about sirens, who they know do not exist. The first-person narrator has taken Malus's place in the old tower, which is now crumbling. A layer of snow or dust or ash covers everything, and the narrator feels as though his body were in a cocoon; he's in bed in his room in his city apartment and does not have much longer to live.

For all the strangeness of *Les Gommes* it is certainly less difficult to comprehend than this oneiric first novel. The disembodied first-person narrative voice speaking for a community which lives in suffering isolated from a better real world which exists perhaps only in imagination recalls the tone and narrative techniques of the Belgian poet Henri Michaux in *Voyage en Grande Garabagne* (1936), *Au Pays de la Magie* (1941), and *Ici, Poddema* (1946), yet in 1948–49 Robbe-Grillet was not familiar with Michaux's work. Similarly the calm and gray setting of the opening of Robert Pinget's *Passacaille* finds an echo in the description of the desolate, mournful island twenty years before the publication of Pinget's novel, one of Robbe-Grillet's favorite pieces of literature. In fact the eerie foreboding atmosphere created by *Un Régicide* is closer to that in the works of Michaux and Pinget than it is to anything Robbe-Grillet wrote subsequently, including even the monotonous and hollow tone of *La Jalousie*. The sense of futility, alienation, and despair are also somewhat reminiscent of Beckett although *Un Régicide* has nothing of Beckett's—or Robbe-Grillet's—sense of humor. Thus, from a certain point of view this first novel is quite different from Robbe-Grillet's later work.

Recurrent Themes

Yet on first glance what is perhaps most striking about *Un Régicide* comes as a result of its unusual publication history, a novel written in 1949 but not published until 1978, when the author's work is known worldwide. This most striking characteristic is the constancy of Robbe-Grillet's interest in certain scenes and other narrative fragments which would reappear throughout his works. The implication is not that Robbe-Grillet returned to this first work for inspiration but rather that certain narrative fragments, shapes, objects, and actions form a fairly permanent set in the author's mind and constitute for him cores of fascination or at least of potential sources which can be tapped for elaboration into the familiar, Robbe-Grilletian fictional networks. The most important names in *Un Régicide* reappear in later novels: Laura, Jean, Aimone (A... in *La Jalousie*), and Boris. Boris and the king finally merge into one figure in the subsequent works, fulfilling Boris's wish to have a unique relationship to the king and even eventually to take his place. Even in this early work Robbe-Grillet plays with the character's names. Aimone becomes Mona, *amie, amande, anémone, mon âme, mon amante.* Boris goes through transformations as well. As he awakens in his first scene and moves through different levels of consciousness, his name solidifies after going through homophonic variants: Maurice, Moritz, and then Boris. The name of the Solitary One, Malus, also bears a homophonic similarity to Boris, and the character of Malus plays a role in relation to the first-person narrator on the island which corresponds to the relationship Boris might wish to establish with the king. Like the king, Malus is a special person; he too lives separated from the rest of the people in a kind of castle, in the lighthouse with the top of its walls crenellated like a king's castle.

More minor characters make their debut in *Un Régicide* as well. The street sweeper from *La Maison de rendez-vous* is already at work in his futile attempt to make a neat pile of the *feuilles* (sheet of paper or leaves in French) on the street. The two somewhat inefficient policemen who come to arrest Boris, only to outdistance him and lose him as they walk through the city, will later arrest Caroline in *Souvenirs du triangle d'or* with similar results. The ubiquitous doctor present in so many of Robbe-Grillet's works is born in *Un Régicide* in a scene which foreshadows and is nearly identical to ones he will play in *Dans le labyrinthe,* visiting a dying patient in his home. The sirens that come to bless the island in summer become the half fish/half woman in *La Belle Captive* but are also transformed into the many mannequins which are tortured, torn apart, and set on fire in later works.

Themes which surface on nearly every page of *Un Régicide* provide further continuity. Communication, for example, is a problem: Boris cannot talk to Laura; the first-person narrator has difficulty expressing his thoughts to his companions; the sirens do not speak the same language as their lovers on the island. Announcements made on the radio playing in the apartment of Boris's neighbors cannot be clearly understood. Boris prefers to get his news from the newspaper, from the written word, where order, linearity, and truth reside. In fact Boris waits to find out from the newspaper whether his attempted assassination of the king actually took place; he is then confused by the newspaper's contradictions not only of his own perceptions and memories of killing the king but also of Laura's statement that the king is dead. In addition to the theme of the impossibility of communication and the untrustworthiness of even the written word, the familiar and hopeless desire for order and causality in a world of confusion finds expression here. Boris's job at the factory is to calculate; he worries constantly about making errors in his calculations at work and in his assassination plot. His speculations and reconstitutions of scenes (past or future scenes) give this text a fabric foreshadowing the multiple scene variations that characterize later Robbe-Grillet texts. The same scene is played over and over or the same group of words is repeated as though the narrative were stuck. Boris's reason for reviewing scenes is to remember them as they truly occurred, but with each repetition variations are introduced so that his speculations drift farther and farther away from the original scenes they were to duplicate, leaving him in an intolerable, insane state of confusion.

Fear of chaos generates frequent references to traps, catastrophes, errors—the same dangers that threaten all of Robbe-Grillet's characters who try to make sense of events and to reconstruct a correct order from the debris of their physical and mental life. Boris's vain attempt to organize his possessions in his room is paralleled by the first-person narrator's attempt to find his way around his native island, where he has lived all his life and every path of which he knows by heart, but where he gets lost because the fog is so dense that he can perceive the world around him only in bits and pieces, never making out an object in its entirety. Similarly the major construction project which is a central issue in the platform of all the political parties in the country was begun with no ultimate goal in mind; the site is a chaotic mix of scaffolding, half-built walls, and hills of sand and debris overrun with weeds, but no one can agree on whether the construction should become a church, a convalescent home, or a series of roads. There is no overall plan, no whole, only bits and pieces. Nonetheless, in all the novels from *Un Régicide* to *Souvenirs du triangle d'or* Robbe-Grillet's characters make vain attempts to impose an order on events which refuse to cooperate.

Failure to organize the world is one of several failures in *Un Régicide*. Robbe-Grillet has said that many of his characters are plagued with an inability to accomplish tasks assigned to them or to achieve their goals:[5] Wallas commits the murder he was sent to investigate; the soldier in *Dans le labyrinthe* never delivers his package; all the characters who try to kill someone in the later novels are plagued by the inexplicable rebirth of their victims. Like so many of Robbe-Grillet's works the beginning of *Un Régicide* is not a beginning but a replay of a scene that has already taken place many times; and the narrator knows it will take place again. His attempt to cross all the rocky, dangerous obstacles in his path and to reach a flat, safe stretch of beach has failed:

". . . once again I will have to cross the whirlpools and the foam. I still have tons of sand to move around . . ." (12).

The new hope in the narrator's life is his discovery of a stranger on the island which no one ever visits. Malus, this wise father figure, knows answers, knows that the sirens will come and bring joy to the island. In the meantime, the narrator's double, Boris, has also found the answer to the problem of isolation and stagnation. He must get close to the king just as the first-person narrator has gotten close to Malus. Boris's first idea is to become the king's servant but he soon realizes that this would make of him only one of many servants. He must establish a unique relationship with the king, the kindly father figure, kill him, and replace him as king. But these two events, the coming of the sirens and the assassination of the king, are linked and develop along parallel lines. If Boris can kill the father-king, the first-person narrator can capture a siren. During his attempt to kill the king, Boris is haunted, almost hypnotized, by scenes from the island in which he, not the first-person narrator, is enjoying the warmth of Aimone. But Malus had warned the first-person narrator not to return to the sirens; when his warning is ignored, he disappears from the text. With the disappearance of Malus comes the apparent death of his double, the king, the return of the unpleasant season on the island, and the final departure of the sirens.

The attempt to change the pattern of daily existence has failed for everyone, for although the king still lives for Boris, he has died for Laura, causing political problems in the country and forcing Laura to leave, like the sirens. Only the first-person narrator seems to have had a measure of success; he now lives in the old watchtower and looks over his island, which he no longer describes in the same negative terms he had used at the beginning. The final task for this first-person narrator is to eliminate Boris from the text as all the others have been suppressed. And in fact whereas Boris and the first-person narrator are quite separate at the beginning of the book, separated into a real life and a dream life, these two characters representing their respective levels of reality begin to merge until at the end Boris disappears altogether and his reality is assumed by the first-person narrator, who now lives in Boris's room, sleeps in Boris's bed. But he too is doomed. He is dying; he cannot continue to live after Boris is suppressed any more than the dream of a better life can survive the death of the king, the disappearance of Malus, and the departure of the sirens. The attempts to kill the father and possess the mother have both failed and once again, like Sisyphus, the narrator finds himself on a rocky coast at dusk.

Oedipal Problems

The clearly Oedipal situation in *Un Régicide* transforms a few years later in *Les Gommes* into references not to an Oedipal complex but to Sophocles' play *Oedipus the King,* in which the structure of the play and the events and characters in it become raw material for Robbe-Grillet's novel. This concentration on Oedipus and his situation is particularly interesting in light of Robbe-Grillet's comments about his mother and the patterns of his psychological relationship to women in "Fragment autobiographique imaginaire," published in *Minuit* at about the same time that *Un Régicide* and *Souvenir du triangle d'or* appeared.[6] No doubt all three of these works, although not written at the same time, were on his mind as he looked them over just before publication. The Breton coast described in "Fragment" is the same one that appears in *Un Régicide* and that had appeared in Robbe-Grillet's recurrent dream, frightening, full of pits into which the rushing waves might draw a person and drown him. In "Fragment," however, he also describes the gentle calming slopes of the Jura region. Both these landscapes are associated with his mother, and Robbe-Grillet preempts Freudian critics by pointing out himself that these two landscapes represent opposing symbolizations of his fear of and desire for woman.

The psychological reading of *Les Gommes* made possible by Morrissette's analysis of the novel's references to the Oedipus myth becomes more compelling with the publication of *Un Régicide* in which father images must be eliminated in order to secure the happiness represented by union with female figures. Robbe-Grillet remembers his relationship to his father as warm and supportive although he acknowledges that allusions to father figures permeate his work and lend support to the argument that much of his work is psychologically rooted in an obsession with Oedipal problems. The fact that Robbe-Grillet used *Oedipus the King* as a source of *Les Gommes* indicates his own awareness early on of the significance of Oedipus to him. Throughout his career he has continued to be aware of and consciously to manipulate his obsessions in his writings. Certainly this manipulation is clear in his treatment of women in the works from his second and third periods in which women are always more or less beautiful, mobile mannequins. In *Souvenirs du triangle d'or* he pays homage to the Oedipal father of *Un Régicide*. Good King Boris reappears surrounded by the black crows which appeared in *Un Régicide;* as the revolutionary insurgents invade the palace to assassinate him, he tries to make their task easier by striking the pose he has in the official portrait of himself, the portrait from *Un Régicide* which Boris kept pinned to his bedroom wall. The father figure knows his role in the Oedipal drama; he must be eliminated.

Un Régicide as Literary Document

The publication of *Un Régicide* only in 1978 creates an interesting perspective on the characters in the novel. Names like Boris and Jean, which Robbe-Grillet chose because they connoted nothing in particular about the personalities of those who bore them, are suddenly charged in another way. They may remain undefined by their connections to the real world but they are defined or limited by the fictional world of Robbe-Grillet which has preceded them and in which their names figure. The king will have recurrent parts to play in the novels and he will become permanently associated with the name Boris. Boris and Jean, which is the king's name in *Un Régicide,* are the two once again merged characters in the film *L'Homme qui ment.* Laura too reappears regularly, sometimes much younger, as in *Projet pour une révolution à New York.* This is not to say that these names refer to characters who play roles in the novels and films but rather that the names themselves carry an intertextual weight, and the reader familiar with Robbe-Grillet is interested to see an early

Laura, Boris, and Jean, before they were so carefully emptied of
"personalities." Nevertheless, even though, for example, the introduction into the novel of Laura and the explanation of her
political views follow the conventions of novel writing, as early
as *Un Régicide* the characters have no past, no physical characteristics, no life outside the descriptions of them in the novel.
From this point of view Robbe-Grillet's handling of his characters
foreshadows his future, more conscious manipulations and already
represents a departure from conventional novel form.

Given that Robbe-Grillet insists on his lack of familiarity with
these conventional novel forms one must conclude that his challenge to them was unintentional, at least in *Un Régicide,* and that
Robbe-Grillet was not concerned in 1949 with problems of narrative technique. If he was nevertheless already playing with word
games, narrative voice, and character development, these deviations from the norm were the result of his admiration for and no
doubt more or less unconscious imitation of writers like Camus
(Boris shares certain characteristics with the Meursault of
L'Etranger, part one), Roussel, and Kafka, writers whose work
he knew.

Yet, if for the most part this novel was written before Robbe-
Grillet began to question how his own literary interests did or
did not correspond to norms, this same innocence does not apply
to the section rewritten in 1957, after Robbe-Grillet had already
published articles on his literary theories, criticizing, for example,
metaphor, literature as political commitment, the idea of the
fixed character with a name, a history, a real life. In 1957 he
had just finished *La Jalousie* and was still in the period of concentration on long, minutely detailed descriptions of objects. One
particularly clear example of the influence of the theories which
were on Robbe-Grillet's mind at the time of the 1957 revisions
occurs in the first few pages of *Un Régicide.* Boris awakes and goes
to shave: "He chose a blade, among those which had already been
used on other days, and attached it to the mechanical razor,
twisting the screw all the way, and then unscrewing it a quarter
of a turn. . . . The index finger of the free hand moved slowly
over the upper gums and teeth from the premolars on one side

to the premolars on the other side in one direction then in the other five or six times" (17–18). The detail, the use of numbers, the dispassion, the precision, the irrelevance of the description to the "plot" of the novel are all reminiscent of the first period of Robbe-Grillet's literary career. It is possible that this description, written so clearly in the style of the Robbe-Grillet of the 1950s, was Robbe-Grillet's tongue-in-cheek tribute to himself; such a tribute would certainly not be out of character. The shaving scene is perhaps also the point at which Robbe-Grillet abandoned his revisions as he realized that to continue them would in effect have meant an entirely new, entirely different novel, for immediately following this description of Boris shaving is the introduction of Laura in a style much less unconventional and not at all typical of Robbe-Grillet's work anywhere but in *Un Régicide.* Boris speculates on his scheduled meeting with Laura and remembers similar meetings in the past; each description is in the appropriate verb tense (conditional for the speculation, imperfect for the past) and there is no confusion of past, present, and future, of real and imaginary, of memory, experience, and speculation which would later become Robbe-Grillet's trademark. Each reality remains on its own plane and the opportunity to disintegrate neat categories of fictional reality is ignored. Yet even in *Un Régicide,* eventually the oneiric plane of the island and Boris's real life in the city do become entangled.

Un Régicide is a fascinating work because it contains so many seeds of the themes and novelistic concerns which were to develop later throughout Robbe-Grillet's work. To the extent that the direction Robbe-Grillet's writing took was influenced by positive and negative critical reaction to it, *Un Régicide* has been a secret treasure for Robbe-Grillet from which he could pull these themes in order to explore them away from the watchful and influential, i.e., capable of making him change direction, eyes of his readers. Serving as an anchor and repository of Robbe-Grillet's literary interests, *Un Régicide* for nearly thirty years held the common roots of works like *Les Gommes, L'Année dernière à Marienbad,* and *Souvenirs du triangle d'or.* Where critics found contradictions in Robbe-Grillet's work, *Un Régicide* is proof of a profound continuity. That the book did not appear for so many years is not a sign of Robbe-Grillet's rejection of a work of his youth but rather a sign of its importance to Robbe-Grillet's conception of his mission in writing. Much of that mission is now literary history. Robbe-Grillet's career is established and deviations from what is perceived by the public to be his style can no longer be called contradictions but rather further developments.

Robbe-Grillet's literary development has gone very far beyond *Un Régicide*. The publication of this book along with the "Fragment," the first few pages of Robbe-Grillet's autobiography, which may or may not ever actually be completed, signals a pause in Robbe-Grillet's career and perhaps a new change in direction necessary for an author whose work has now become part of the canon and who therefore intends to find a new way to challenge his readers and to challenge those conceptions of literature which he himself did so much to create in the 1950s and 1960s. The concept of the author, from whom truth flows, was challenged during that period; for some the author became merely the *scripteur*. The *scripteur* is now being challenged in turn. There is no reason to allow the author to remain transparent merely because he has become so, for theory has never dictated creation for Robbe-Grillet. Interest in an author's biography, his psychology, his literary history is once again finding favor as a valid approach to literature. In fact, Robbe-Grillet seems to be encouraging such an approach since, as he says in "Fragments," "I have never spoken about anything but myself. Since it was from the inside, it was scarcely noticeable."[7] *Un Régicide* is a glimpse into this inside.

Chapter Eleven
The Films

In 1959 producer Samy Halfon and musician Michel Fano approached Robbe-Grillet with the possibility of doing a film. Although he had been interested in the idea of making a film for some time, Robbe-Grillet felt that he had to warn Halfon and Fano that the type of creative work that interested him was unlikely to attract the massive audiences necessary to make a film a financial success. Fortunately, Halfon and Fano were interested in experimental cinema and this proposed collaboration began Robbe-Grillet's career as a cinematographer. One stipulation was that this film had to be shot in Turkey for financial reasons, a stipulation which in fact did not displease Robbe-Grillet as he knew Istanbul well. As a crossroads between Eastern and Western civilizations, Istanbul was a city which existed in the minds of Westerners as mysterious and exotic, conjuring images of drug trade, harems, and white slave trade that fascinated Robbe-Grillet and provided him with the type of mythologically charged climate that Robbe-Grillet enjoyed manipulating. He began his script for *L'Immortelle,* but before the film could be shot, political problems in the country forced a suspension of work. In the meantime, however, director Alain Resnais, already quite well known for *Hiroshima, mon amour,* was looking for a script for a new movie, and a collaboration between Resnais and Robbe-Grillet was proposed. In 1960, therefore, Robbe-Grillet wrote the scenario for *L'Année dernière à Marienbad.* A resolution of the situation in Turkey then allowed the continuation of work on *L'Immortelle,* which Robbe-Grillet himself directed, leaving the filming of *L'Année* entirely to Resnais. Thus, *L'Année,* although the second scenario written, was the first film to appear in movie houses in 1961, *L'Immortelle* first appearing two years later in 1963.

To many of his readers cinema seemed an obvious medium for Robbe-Grillet; his insistence in his texts up to 1960 on the surfaces of objects and their geometric shapes, his *école du regard*, his refusal to assume the role of omniscient author aware of the thoughts and motivations of his characters, and his interests expressed in his theoretical writings in the distancing effect of vision made readers think of his books as a kind of cinema of words. In fact Robbe-Grillet's films, like his books, display a continuing concern with manipulations of narrative in which chronology is distorted, contradictory "facts" are abundant, reality is not represented, characters have little psychological depth.

There is a general theoretical and sensual continuity from his novels to his films. From the beginning, however, and, increasingly, as he continued his work in films, it became apparent to Robbe-Grillet that the creation of a film and the creation of a novel are two entirely different processes. The desire to write begins with the insistent pressure of words and phrases on the author's imagination, while images, not words, push his creative imagination toward films. Furthermore, a scenario even complete with details on camera positions and sound track is relatively rapidly achieved, while Robbe-Grillet works painstakingly slowly on his novels, producing only a very few pages a day.[1]

But the most significant difference for Robbe-Grillet lies in the fact that a writer works alone, grappling only with obstacles that arise from his own creative imagination whereas the bulk of the work done on a film involves not only other people, actors, cameramen, producers, but also objective reality itself, the reality of the objects used in the films and of the locations for the films. The cinematographer must be capable of incorporating these obstacles into his creative plan, because eliminating them is simply not possible; the restrictions imposed, and in some cases the possibilities created, by objective reality must in effect serve as creative generators, as part of the givens which the filmmaker must use in the creation of his own statement. In the *ciné-roman* for *Glissements progressifs du plasir,* Robbe-Grillet refers to Saussure's distinction between *langue* and *parole*. From the relatively limited stock of elements available in the *langue,* actors, locations, real objects, the cinematographer chooses and manipulates those with which he intends to make his *parole.*

For Robbe-Grillet the very resistance of these necessary outside elements has come to constitute part of the excitement of film-making and is the reason behind his insistence on shooting only on location and not necessarily excluding from the footage accidents which may occur on the set, such as people walking by on the street, staring at the camera, or even asking for autographs. Robbe-Grillet's approach has been to allow the film to grow out of this external reality. Thus, for example, the film *L'Homme qui ment* (1968) came into being to fit a locale which Robbe-Grillet found interesting, the Carpathian forests separating Poland, the Ukraine, and Czechoslovakia. The stark blue and white of the towns in Tunisia under the blazing sun played a role of major importance in the serial generation of *L'Eden et après* (1970). The location where a film is to be shot simply must be decided in advance, if only for financial reasons, and cannot be generated by the writing itself, as is possible in novels, such as Ricardou's *Les Lieux dits.*

Another aspect of filmmaking which separates it from novel writing, and one in which Robbe-Grillet has been able to make important innovations, is the role of the sound track. Robbe-Grillet's fascination with modern, experimental music preceded his interest in literature and his use of musical structures, already present in his novels in the form of themes and variations, culminates in *L'Eden et après,* in which thematic elements are combined in formal series as in dodecaphonic music. Traditionally, the three parts of a film sound track, words, noises, and music, are arranged to supplement the core of the movie, which is the images on the screen. Thus, romantic music is heard during tender love scenes, the sound of a gunshot is heard when a gun is being shot off on the screen, and the dialogue is always directly related to the actions shown on the screen at the moment. This redundancy of the sound track radically undermines its importance, makes the sound track essentially irrelevant, the images providing all the basic information necessary for the understanding of the film. Robbe-Grillet on the other hand takes advantage of the sound track's potential for providing information of its own and the sound track takes on an importance equal to that of the images on the screen by developing, linking, and, most important, contesting those images.[2] Michel Fano, an award-winning composer, has collaborated with Robbe-Grillet on the sound tracks of all his films.

Finally, a very basic and important difference between film and literature is the process by which the viewer or reader receives the work. The reader's participation in the work he is reading is necessarily active, particularly when the work in question is of the type Robbe-Grillet produces. Furthermore, the reader is likely to reread sections, for pleasure or for better understanding, and he may skip sections. The thought processes set off by reading a text may take place at intervals during the reading. Reactions to a film, however, must wait until the film has been seen in its entirety or the viewer runs the risk of missing segments of the film as he thinks about what he has just seen. Viewing a film is generally quite passive; the viewer, as Robbe-Grillet says, submits to the film. He is more manipulated, much less in control of the process itself of absorbing the film. Freud felt that the very nature of the enormous image in a dark room constitutes a kind of aggression against the viewer. His vision and sense of hearing are entirely taken up, uninterruptedly, by the film and normally within a community of viewers in which the reactions of others in the darkened auditorium potentially have some impact on the individual's understanding or appreciation of the film.

The appreciation of the film by the general public can in fact be the prime factor in determining whether a film will continue to be available. If the film attracts no audience, it will not be shown. Public reaction poses particularly grave problems for an experimental filmmaker like Robbe-Grillet, whose novels were termed unreadable when they first appeared. General acceptance of each of Robbe-Grillet's novels took some time, the latest novel at first always being judged to be inferior by comparison with the previous ones, which themselves had at first also been criticized. This almost inevitable delay in public acceptance of an experimental work can be disastrous for a film, which must become a success in a matter of weeks in order to survive.

Because of this problematic availability of the film and because particularly interesting or difficult parts of the film cannot normally be played back, Robbe-Grillet decided to publish the scenarios of his films, complete with technical details of camera angles, lighting, etc., so that those interested in studying a film in detail might do so just as a concertgoer might read the score of a piece of music; neither the score nor the *ciné-roman* is a substitute for the real work of art, the music or the film. The *ciné-roman* for *L'Année* and *L'Immortelle* posed no problem for Robbe-Grillet because for these two films he had written out the entire scenarios before the film was shot, the films becoming fairly exact filmic duplicates of these screenplays. After *L'Immortelle,* however, the scenarios became increasingly brief, and it was during the actual shooting that the films took form. Thus Robbe-Grillet had nothing to publish unless, based on the film already in existence, he simply recopied on paper what was already on the celluloid. The problem for Robbe-Grillet in this reproduction is obvious. Loath to representing reality in his films and books, Robbe-Grillet's temptation in writing a posteriori a scenario for a film is to challenge and distort the elements of the film so that the scenario would contest the film and thereby undermine the original purpose of the scenario. There are, therefore, no *ciné-romans* of the other Robbe-Grillet films: *Trans-Europ-Express* (1967), *L'Homme qui ment, L'Eden et après, N a pris les dés* (1971),[3] or *Le Jeu avec le feu* (1975). The only other *ciné-roman, Glissements progressifs du plaisir* (1974), includes the script upon which the film is based plus all modifications made in the script during the filming. Other projects for films were never produced, including recently a film to be called *Piège à fourrure.* Like *L'Eden,* the film would develop according to a serial pattern incorporating generative themes surrounding a basic situation.[4]

Unfortunately experimental cinema like Robbe-Grillet's is having a difficult time surviving. Funds are not easy to find for any film at a time when television is emptying movie houses. Furthermore, despite the relative popularity of, for example, *Trans-*

Europ-Express, and the artistic quality of *L'Homme qui ment,* Robbe-Grillet's films are not particularly successful; very few cinematographers seem to be interested in pursuing the types of experiments he is interested in; critics in general continue to consider him a novelist who should stick to writing and leave cinema to real filmmakers; and finally, Robbe-Grillet still has an extremely small audience among the general public. Accusations that he is including ever more erotic elements in his films to attract an audience are particularly uninformed since those who would go to see his films especially for their prurient appeal are infuriated by the disjointed narrative, and at least some of those interested in such manipulations of structures and challenges to the cinema code are put off by the display of what they consider Robbe-Grillet's personal sado-erotic fantasies.[5] Nevertheless, Robbe-Grillet's films enjoy some success in certain movie houses in neighborhoods where the clientele are interested in experimentation; Robbe-Grillet claims, for example, that scenes which evoke no reactions in certain movie houses create uproarious laughter in the Latin Quarter in Paris. Perhaps, as it happened with his novels, a public that does not now exist will eventually be created for his films.[6]

Chapter Twelve

Conclusion

The first New Novels of the early 1950s including those of Robbe-Grillet were modernist, that is, oriented toward exploiting the conflict between subjective and objective reality. In addition, for Robbe-Grillet the period up to the middle 1950s was one of defiance of the established order, polemics on what a novel must do and how the novel must change. During this time Robbe-Grillet was, in a sense, out to change the world. From the beginning of his reflections on literature he based his thought on the premise that there is no human nature which defines and therefore restricts man to a certain predetermined and inevitable fate. Nevertheless his earliest theoretical writings posited an opposition between two fundamental and functionally definable entities, man and the world, and Robbe-Grillet seemed to place a certain amount of faith in the capacity of science, of measurement, of surface description to delineate a true or at least somehow stable relationship between the two.

But the subjective/objective debates became irrelevant to Robbe-Grillet's thought when he moved into a postmodernist phase in which his works, no longer content merely to designate themselves as fictions, now began to generate themselves. Once the objective/subjective debate was left behind, narrative structures became the most interesting facets of Robbe-Grillet's work. Personal myths of sado-eroticism emerged as one of his most central themes; his work became more obviously playful and humorous, displaying at the same time a fascination for the urban world of Western civilization, its fantasies, preoccupations, perversions, and fears. In 1961 Robbe-Grillet had postulated the emergence of an *"homme nouveau"* but the new man Robbe-Grillet had hoped for was not to represent a synthesis of the opposing

166

poles of subjective-objective but rather would be the man willing to accept meaning in the world as "partial, provisional, contradictory even, and always challenged."[1] Robbe-Grillet's work began to seek to prevent the immobilization of meaning and to produce instead a multiplication of meaning.

The shift in orientation in Robbe-Grillet's work is paralleled by a similar shift in the orientation of the French intelligentsia since the 1950s. Hegelian and Marxist dialectics and the binary oppositions of Structuralist thought have become increasingly less operative as means of organizing man's perception of his relationship with the world. Even less appealing to philosophers like Jacques Derrida, social philosophers like Michel Foucault, psychoanalysts like Jacques Lacan, or literary critics like Roland Barthes, all of whose works have become dominant influences on recent French intellectual life, is the possibility of the synthesis of contradictions, the notion that there exists a final single Truth, graspable or ungraspable, in relation to which man orients himself. For these post-Structuralist thinkers there is no human nature, no *subjet foundateur* ("founding subject"), no ultimate source that guarantees man his place in the world. Meaning is plural and eternally open-ended. Robbe-Grillet's literature, as well as the evolution of his theoretical positions, clearly reflects this more generalized movement in French thought. Robbe-Grillet's name might be added to those of this group of thinkers described by John Sturrock: "All these thinkers are against authority, and against metaphysics. They do not wish to transcend what they see, in pursuit of some hidden, ultimate meaning which would 'explain' everything; they do not believe that everything can be explained. Nor do they hold with teleological interpretations of history. They are against the singular and for the plural, preferring whole galaxies of meanings to emerge from a limited set of phenomena to the notion that it must hold one, unifying, dominant meaning. They believe, where meaning is concerned, in 'dissemination.' . . ."[2]

At twenty Robbe-Grillet became an agricultural engineer, at thirty a novelist, at forty a cinematographer; at fifty Robbe-Grillet began to work seriously on painting, his collaborations with artists in his latest work reflecting this interest; for his sixties he talks about concentrating on music. An energetic and entertaining presence, Robbe-Grillet has been invited throughout his literary career to explain his research on literature in public forums. He continues to attend many of the summer conferences on literary and intellectual trends at Cerisy-la-Salle near his country home in Normandy whenever the subject under discussion interests him; and Robbe-Grillet is a man of broad interests, who has, for example, never really abandoned his fascination with plants and makes a point of observing the flora around him wherever he travels. Because of his lively personality he is also much sought after for interviews and grants them readily, not always repeating exactly the same truth exactly the same way each time. Robbe-Grillet has probably been able to exercise his influence on contemporary literature most efficiently as literary editor of Les Editions de Minuit, always supporting for publication novels of experimentation.

At the moment interest in the experiments of the Nouveaux Romanciers or the Nouveaux Nouveaux Romanciers has waned in France, and it is not clear that Robbe-Grillet's present literary work, in particular the exploration of his very personal erotic myths, will produce anything like the impact his earlier works did. His body of readers is small but stable; however, his later works have not, at least as yet, attained the status of essential reading which his early works attained. As Robbe-Grillet himself readily points out, the splash made by the Nouveau Roman was at first an effect of journalism; discussions and debates surrounding the Nouveau Roman were fashionable. Nevertheless, despite the decline in attention paid to this literature in the general press and the difficulty in determining what the ultimate importance of the Nouveau Roman and the work of Robbe-Grillet will be, no novelist in France can ignore the innovations and the challenges Robbe-Grillet's work has made to literature; no anthology of modern writers can not include Robbe-Grillet; no assessment of modern literature can avoid coming to grips with his contributions. As Michel Foucault puts it, "Robbe-Grillet's importance is to be measured by the question which his work puts to any work contemporary with it."[3] Whether or not Robbe-Grillet's impact is merely the result of the proper conjuncture of individual, time, and place, largely because of his work, no serious writers can write in the same way as they did before the advent of Robbe-Grillet.

Notes and References

Chapter One

1. Maurice Blanchot, *Le Livre à venir* (Paris: Gallimard, 1959), p. 287.

2. *Archives du XXeme siècle—Alain Robbe-Grillet,* videocassette, Centre Pompidou, Paris, tape 1.

3. In response to this article, Robbe-Grillet wrote Henriot an extremely polite letter in which he pointed out that the very things Henriot criticized in the text formed part of Robbe-Grillet's endeavor to revolutionize not only the novel form but man's very relationship to the world.

4. *Archives du XXeme siècle—Alain Robbe-Grillet,* tape 1.

5. Bruce Morrissette, *The Novels of Robbe-Grillet* (Ithaca, N.Y., 1975), p. 23.

6. Alain Robbe-Grillet, "God on the Quad, Objectivity and Subjectivity in the Nouveau Roman," *New Hungarian Quarterly,* no. 22 (Summer 1966), p. 77.

Chapter Two

1. *The Erasers,* tr. Richard Howard (New York, 1964). Henceforth all references to this work will be incorporated into the text.

2. Morrissette, *Novels,* pp. 38–74.

3. Alain Robbe-Grillet, *Pour un nouveau roman* (Paris, 1963), p. 65.

4. Olga Bernal, *Alain Robbe-Grillet: le roman de l'absence* (Paris, 1964), p. 52–57.

5. *Les Gommes* is actually based not on the myth of Oedipus but on Sophocles' play *Oedipus Rex.*

6. Stephen Heath, in *The Nouveau Roman: A Study in the Practice of Writing* (London, 1972), sees the multiple interpretation of the illegible word in the note as "a short history of the presence of the text in Robbe-Grillet . . . , that in the trajectory of its variants almost sketches an itinerary of Robbe-Grillet's writing," p. 132.

7. See Lucien Goldmann's comments on reification and the fetish of merchandise in *Pour une sociologie du roman* (Paris, 1964), p. 189.

8. *Colloque de Cerisy, Robbe-Grillet* (Paris: 10/18, 1976), 1:133.

9. Ibid., p. 136.

10. Jean Ricardou, "La Population des miroirs," *Poétique* 22 (1975): 202.

11. Bernal, *Alain Robbe-Grillet,* p. 39.

Chapter Three

1. *Le Voyeur* (Paris, 1955). Henceforth all references to this work will be incorporated into the text.

2. The same concern for systems is duplicated at the level of narration as well. For example, Robbe-Grillet regularly puts items in the book together in series of twos and threes: Mme Leduc has three daughters; there are three men drinking at the Café de l'Espérance. Mathias tries three times to fix his bicycle; then his chain slips three times. The ferry blows three whistles before leaving, and there are numerous further examples.

3. Robbe-Grillet's original title for *Le Voyeur* was *La Vue* (*Nouveau Roman: hier, aujourd'hui* [Paris: 10/18, 1972], 1:122), then *Le Voyageur*. Jean Ricardou points out that the suppressed crime in *Le Voyeur* reflects the suppression of the two middle letters of *Le Voy(ag)eur*, in a sense condemning Mathias to change from the *voyageur* (the innocent traveling salesman) to the *voyeur* (*Nouveau Roman: hier, aujourd'hui* [Paris: 10/18, 1972], 2:136–37).

Chapter Four

1. *Jealousy,* tr. Richard Howard (New York, 1959). Henceforth all references to this work will be incorporated into the text.

2. Jacques Leenhardt, *Lecture politique du roman* (Paris, 1973), p. 28.

3. The use of an omniscient narrator guarantees the existence of an ultimate truth, which the narrator knows and parts of which the narrator communicates to the reader. Robbe-Grillet rejects the notion of the existence of such an ultimate truth and such a *sujet fondateur* ("originating subject"). The first-person narrator can only give his own provisional truth.

4. Blanchot, *Le Livre,* p. 241.

5. Leenhardt, *Lecture,* pp. 25–26.

6. In "Nature, humanisme, tragédie," published in 1958, Robbe-Grillet discusses the cleansing function of vision, which cannot penetrate into the profound, anthropomorphic meanings traditional readers generally place behind objects, and which remains rather on the meaningless surface. Already in *La Jalousie,* from 1957, however, the function of vision, while not one of penetration, was not innocent description either.

7. Leenhardt, *Lecture,* p. 51.

8. Quoted in Bernal, *Alain Robbe-Grillet,* p. 205.

9. Leenhardt, *Lecture,* pp. 49–50.

Chapter Five

1. *Dans le labyrinthe* (Paris, 1959). Henceforth all references to this work will be incorporated into the text. Despite Ricardou's statement Robbe-Grillet has pointed out that the very title of *La Jalousie* and a good bit of the thrust of the whole novel repose on a metaphor (*Colloque de Cerisy—Alain Robbe-Grillet,* 1:35).

2. Heath, *Nouveau Roman,* p. 139.

3. Gérard Genette, "Vertige fixé," *Dans le labyrinthe,* pp. 273–310, explains the radical newness of a Robbe-Grillet novel like *Dans le labyrinthe* as the result of Robbe-Grillet's use of paradigmatic structures syntagmatically. In traditional prose, scenes and sequences are linked syntagmatically, i.e., by their contiguity in time and space. Robbe-Grillet's technique is to take paradigmatic sequences, i.e., the possible variations of scenes, and, instead of rejecting all but one and linking that one to its logical successor, to present the entire paradigm, causing the elements of the paradigm to follow each other instead of substituting for each other and thus creating, as Genette says, "those narratives moving nowhere, hesitant, as though suggested and then crossed out, indefinitely interrupted and taken up again" (301).

4. The half-erased contours belong to a whole series of such forms in *Dans le labyrinthe* described using certain privileged words: indistinct, blurred, half-erased, faded. In opposition to this series is another indicating stiffness: uniform, unalterable, rigid, immobile, fixed.

5. In the first mention of this man he is referred to with the definite rather than the indefinite article. The appearance of the definite article in this first mention fits Robbe-Grillet's theoretical comments from this period. The reader will not be interested in a novel merely about forms. "The man" had to appear because he was expected by the reader, who wants to read only about himself. With the simple use of the

definite article Robbe-Grillet reemphasizes the importance of the role of the reader; it was the reader's desire which caused the appearance of the man, the reader's double, his brother.

Chapter Six

1. *La Maison de Rendez-Vous,* tr. Richard Howard (New York, 1966). Henceforth all references to this work will be incorporated into the text.
2. It might be pointed out that the final version of the death of Manneret corresponds fairly closely to the final appearance of King Boris, both occurring in the very last pages of the book, the representatives of the creative imagination eliminated at the same time that the text ends.
3. Alain Robbe-Grillet, "For a Voluptuous Tomorrow," tr. Richard Howard, *Saturday Review,* 20 May 1972, pp. 44–46.
4. Interview with Pierre Demeron, "A Voyeur in the Labyrinth," tr. Richard Howard, *Evergreen Review* 43 (October 1966):46–49.

Chapter Seven

1. *Project for a Revolution in New York,* tr. Richard Howard (New York, 1972). Henceforth all references to this work will be incorporated into the text.
2. Leaflet inserted into French edition of novel, *Projet pour une révolution à New York.*
3. Ibid.
4. Francois Jost, *Colloque de Cerisy—Alain Robbe-Grillet,* discussion, 1:93.
5. Jean Ricardou, *Pour une théorie du nouveau roman* (Paris, 1971), p. 225.
6. The ink blob is interesting because it inevitably points to writing, the writing of this very text, for example, and thereby suggests a simultaneity of reading and writing; the ink blob appears as the author writes the text, but it appears on the finished product of the very text he is in the process of writing. This simultaneity reflects Robbe-Grillet's method of writing, constantly reading from the beginning the text he is producing. See "Comment travaillent les écrivains," *Le Monde,* 16 January 1976, p. 17.
7. The noises act as conduits among narrative spaces. The click of the subway wheels suggesting the click of a door lock allows Laura to escape from the house into the subway scenes.

8. Ricardou, *Pour une théorie,* pp. 223–24.

9. Insert, *Projet pour une révolution à New York.*

10. Included in the program of torture arranged for JR is an intermission during which she will prepare a little snack for her assassin. Similarly Laura's torture, which never actually surfaces in the text, is said to be interrupted while her tormentors go down to the next subway station for a bite to eat, a raw beef sandwich and a cocaine lemonade. Roger Shattuck calls this censorship of announced violence literary *coitus interruptus.*

11. Insert, *Projet pour une révolution à New York.*

12. Susan Suleiman, "Reading Robbe-Grillet: Sadism and Text in *Projet pour une révolution à New York,*" *Romanic Review,* no. 1 (1977), pp. 43–62.

13. Insert, *Projet pour une révolution à New York.*

14. *Colloque de Cerisy—Alain Robbe-Grillet,* 1:216.

Chapter Eight

1. *Topology of a Phantom City,* tr. J. A. Underwood (New York: Grove Press, 1977). Henceforth all references to this work will be incorporated into the text.

2. Interview with Katherine Passias, "New Novel, New New Novel," *Substance,* no. 13 (1976), p. 130.

3. Raymond Queneau's *Le Chiendent* talks about the perverse pleasure one of the characters takes in watching what he calls the construction of ruins. This theme had also appeared in Robbe-Grillet's film *L'Immortelle.*

4. *Colloque de Cerisy—Alain Robbe-Grillet,* 1:36.

5. Alain Robbe-Grillet, "Order and Disorder in Film and Fiction," tr. Bruce Morrissette, *Critical Inquiry,* Autumn 1977, pp. 1–20.

6. The reference here to this 1967 criticism of the New Novel is interesting. The early unreadable texts Boisdeffre criticized have not only become readable but are also now part of the literary canon of the twentieth century.

7. This particular collaboration with Hamilton began when Robbe-Grillet was asked to write an introduction to Hamilton's work for an exhibition of his photographs in Germany. For a detailed history of the publication of all these texts, see Bruce Morrissette, *Intertextual Assemblages in Robbe-Grillet from Topology to the Golden Triangle* (Fredericton, N.B., 1977).

8. Bruce Morrissette, "Intertextual Assemblage as Fictional Generator: *Topologic d'une cité fantôme,*" *International Fiction Review,* 5 (1):5–6.

9. Interview with Jeanine Warnod, "Rencontres—Paul Delvaux et Alain Robbe-Grillet," *Figaro Littéraire,* no. 1507 (5 April 1975), p. 1.

10. Only forty copies of the $6,000 book were published, each copy signed by both the artist and the writer.

11. *La Belle Captive* (Paris, 1975), back cover.

12. For a very helpful discussion of the circulation of meaning between image and text see François Jost, "Le Picto-roman," *Revue d'Esthétique; Voir, entendre* (Paris: 10/18, 1976), pp. 58–73.

13. In another example of how Robbe-Grillet includes novel theory and critics into the fabric of his work, the narrator in *Topologie* is a Ricardolian ideal, organizing his text around forms and letters.

14. Françoise Meltzer, "Preliminary Excavations of Robbe-Grillet's Phantom City," *Chicago Review,* Summer 1976, pp. 41–50.

15. In her excellent article on *Topologie* Françoise Meltzer finds even more of these generating bits; an isosceles triangle is also the Greek letter delta, which helps produce David, a symmetrical name that is therefore visually bisexual. She discusses the transformations of the letters G and H as well as the importance of other geometrical figures, the ovoid, the rectangle, the cube (made of two isosceles triangles).

16. See Morrissette, *Intertextual Assemblages,* p. 54, for an additional lettristic transformation: *gravide* into Gradiva, the name of the principal female character of the Wilhelm Jensen short story *Gradiva* (1904), a text well known to the Surrealists and known to Robbe-Grillet.

17. *Colloque de Cerisy—Alain Robbe-Grillet,* 1:324.

Chapter Nine

1. *Souvenirs du triangle d'or* (Paris, 1978). Henceforth all references to this work will be incorporated into the text. The book's first title was *Propriétés secrètes du triangle.* The triangular form is a privileged shape which can be exploited, as Robbe-Grillet says, for its physical characteristics, its sexual connotations, and its mythical potential. Interview with Michel Rybalka, *Le Monde,* 22 September 1978.

2. Some of Robbe-Grillet's collages appear in *Obliques,* no. 16–17, ed. François Jost (1978).

3. The erotic nature of these pictures of children (many of them pictures of Mme Ionesco's young daughter) led to the book's being

censured in France. Although the book is available in bookstores in France, it is not easy to find.

4. Interview with Rybalka.

5. This is a reference to *Un Régicide*, published at the same time as *Souvenirs*.

6. See Morrissette's interesting discussion of *hasard objectif* in *Intertextual Assemblages*, p. 45 and following, in which he discusses in detail the astonishing number of items upon which Magritte, Rauschenberg, and Johns in particular had focused their attention before their contacts with Robbe-Grillet (in the case of Magritte, never having collaborated with Robbe-Grillet) and which overlapped with Robbe-Grillet's own obsessions—Magritte's men who look like proper bourgeois doctors, the assassins, the foot fetish; Rauschenberg's bulls; Johns's numbers.

Chapter Ten

1. *Un Régicide* (Paris, 1978). Henceforth all references to this work will be incorporated into the text. *Dans le labyrinthe* comes closest to reproducing the dreamlike quality of the text although even in *Les Gommes* certain scenes recall the slow or suspended movement of *Un Régicide;* yet, the more fantastic sections of *Les Gommes* were overlooked. Thus, when *L'Année dernière à Marienbad* appeared on the screen in 1961, critics interpreted the fantasy apparent in this film as a turning point in Robbe-Grillet's career. In fact his interest in fantasy dated from his earliest, although then unknown, work.

2. Robbe-Grillet recounts the following interesting incident in connection with the rejection of *Un Régicide*. After the publication of *Les Gommes*, Robbe-Grillet was contacted by Dominique Audry, to whom he had originally submitted his *Régicide* manuscript. She requested that he return to Gallimard the letter of rejection of his manuscript so that she might verify something in the letter. A year or so later when Robbe-Grillet asked that Gallimard return the letter to him, he was told that he had never submitted a book to Gallimard for publication and that there was therefore no letter of rejection (*Archives du XXème siècle*, tape 1).

3. Interview with Rybalka.

4. Denise Bourdet, "Le Cas de Robbe-Grillet," *La Revue de Paris*, no. 66 (January 1959), p. 133.

5. Interview with Rybalka.

6. *Minuit*, no. 31 (November 1978).

7. Ibid., p. 2.

Chapter Eleven

1. Robbe-Grillet tells the story of his work on *La Jalousie*. Henri Gouin provided him with two servants and the Royaumont Abbey so that he might concentrate entirely without disturbance on his writing. When Gouin reappeared after three months, he was shocked to find that in spite of having worked continuously, Robbe-Grillet had managed to produce a total of only seven pages! ("Comment travaillent les écrivains," p. 17).

2. A simple example would be a scene which occurs in *L'Homme qui ment* in which Jean-Louis Trintignant pretends to drop an imaginary glass and the sound track registers the sound of a glass breaking; or, vice versa, Trintignant drops a real glass but nothing resembling a glass breaking occurs in the sound track.

3. This film, made especially for television, uses many yards of footage shot for *L'Eden et après* but which were not used and shots and even entire sequences which were used in *L'Eden* itself. The title is an anagram of *L'Eden et après*.

4. A description of the basic structure of this film appears in *Minuit*, no. 18 (1978).

5. Film critic Roy Armes, for example, liked *L'Homme qui ment* but was very disappointd with *Le Jeu avec le feu* for this very reason. Roy Armes, "Playing with Fire," *London Magazine*, no. 2 (January to June 1975), pp. 87–90.

6. A more detailed discussion of the individual films is beyond the scope of this study. Furthermore, Robbe-Grillet's importance as a cinematographer is not comparable to the impact he has had on French letters. Nevertheless, he has made almost as many films as he has written novels and the reader is referred to the studies of Robbe-Grillet's films noted in the bibliography.

Chapter Twelve

1. *Pour un nouveau roman*, pp. 151–52.

2. John Sturrock, ed., *Structuralism and Since* (Oxford: Oxford University Press, 1979), p. 15.

3. Michel Foucault, "Distance, Aspect, Origine," in *Théorie d'ensemble* (Paris: Editions du Seuil, 1968), p. 11.

Selected Bibliography

PRIMARY SOURCES

(First editions only indicated)

Les Gommes. Paris: Les Editions de Minuit, 1953.
 The Erasers. Translated by Richard Howard. New York: Grove Press, 1964.
Le Voyeur. Paris: Les Editions de Minuit, 1955.
 The Voyeur. Translated by Richard Howard. New York: Grove Press, 1958.
La Jalousie. Paris: Les Editions de Minuit, 1957.
 Jealousy. Translated by Richard Howard. New York: Grove Press, 1959.
Dans le labyrinthe. Paris, Les Editions de Minuit, 1959.
 In the Labyrinth. Translated by Richard Howard. New York: Grove Press, 1960.
L'Année dernière à Marienbad (ciné-roman). Paris: Les Editions de Minuit, 1961.
 Last Year at Marienbad. Translated by Richard Howard. New York: Grove Press, 1962.
Instantanés. Paris: Les Editions de Minuit, 1962.
 Snapshots: Stories by Alain Robbe-Grillet. Translated by Bruce Morrissette. New York: Grove Press, 1968.
Pour un nouveau roman (essays). Paris: Les Editions de Minuit, 1963.
 For a New Novel: Essays on Fiction. Translated by Richard Howard. New York: Grove Press, 1965.
L'Immortelle (ciné-roman). Paris: Les Editions de Minuit, 1963.
 The Immortal One. Translated by Alan M. Sheridan-Smith. London: Calder and Boyars, 1971.
La Maison de rendez-vous. Paris: Les Editions de Minuit, 1965.
 La Maison de Rendez-vous. Translated by Richard Howard. New York: Grove Press, 1966.

Projet pour une révolution à New York. Paris: Les Editions de Minuit, 1970.
   Project for a Revolution in New York. Translated by Richard Howard. New York: Grove Press, 1972.
Rêves de jeunes filles. Paris: Laffont, 1971. Text by Robbe-Grillet; photographs by David Hamilton.
   Dreams of a Young Girl. New York: Morrow, 1971.
Les Demoiselles d'Hamilton. Paris: Laffont, 1972. Text by Robbe-Grillet; photographs by David Hamilton.
   Sisters. Translated by Martha Egan. New York: Morrow, 1973.
Glissements progressifs du plaisir (ciné-roman). Paris: Les Editions de Minuit, 1974.
Construction d'un temple en ruine à la déesse Vanadé. Paris: Le Bateau-Lavoir, 1975 (limited edition). Text by Robbe-Grillet; etchings and engravings by Paul Delvaux.
Topologie d'une cité fantôme. Paris: Les Editions de Miniut, 1975.
   Topology of a Phantom City. Translated by J. A. Underwood. New York: Grove Press, 1977.
La Belle Captive. Paris: La Bibliothèque des arts, 1975 (limited edition). Text by Robbe-Grillet; paintings by René Magritte.
Traces suspectes en surface. New York: Tatyana Grosman, Universal Limited Art Editions, 1978 (limited edition). Text by Robbe-Grillet; lithographs by Robert Rauschenberg. Only 40 copies of the book were printed, each signed by both contributors.
Souvenirs du triangle d'or. Paris: Les Editions de Minuit, 1978.
Un Régicide. Paris: Les Editions de Minuit, 1978. (Text written in 1949.)
"Fragment autobiographique imaginaire." *Minuit,* no. 31 (November 1978):2–8.
Le Rendez-vous. New York: Holt, Rinehart, Winston, 1981. Intermediate-level French textbook; text by Robbe-Grillet; grammatical exercises by Yvone Lenard.
Djinn, un trou rouge entre les pavés disjoints. Paris: Les Editions de Minuit, 1981. Same text as *Le Rendez-vous.*

SECONDARY SOURCES

Alter, Jean. *La Vision du monde d'Alain Robbe-Grillet. Structures et significations.* Genève: Librairie Droz, 1966. Covers *Les Gommes* to *La*

Maison de rendez-vous. Alter analyzes the structures in these novels and explores the implications of oppostons like liberty-fatality, order-disorder for outlining a Robbe-Grilletian metaphysics.

Barthes, Roland. *Essais critiques.* Paris: Editions du Seuil, 1964. Particularly important for Robbe-Grillet are three articles: "Littérature littérale," 1955, on *Le Voyeur;* "Littérature objective," 1954, on *Les Gommes;* "Le Point sur Robbe-Grillet," 1962, written as the preface to Morrissette's study of Robbe-Grillet, contesting Morrissette's point of view, and postulating two Robbe-Grillets.

Bernal, Olga. *Alain Robbe-Grillet: le roman de l'absence.* Paris: Gallimard, 1964. Excellent study of absences, holes, missing parts from *Les Gommes* through *Dans le labyrinthe* focusing on the phenomenological aspects of the works.

Brochier, J. J. Interview. "Robbe-Grillet: mes romans, mes films et mes ciné-romans." *Magazine Littéraire,* no. 6 (April 1967), pp. 10–20. Discussion of critical reception of the early novels and films through *Trans-Europ-Express.* Anecdotal but particularly helpful for an understanding of Robbe-Grillet's intentions and procedures in the production of the films.

Dumur, Guy. Interview. "Le Sadisme contre la peur." *Le Nouvel Observateur,* 19–25 October 1970, pp. 47–49. Robbe-Grillet comments mainly on *Projet pour une révolution à New York,* explaining the importance in his works of images of terror, repulsion, and sadistic eroticism treated with humor.

Ferrire, J.-L., Collange, C., Chapsal, M., and Billard, P. Interview. "L'Express va plus loin avec Alain Robbe-Grillet." *L'Express,* 1–7 April 1968, pp. 142–75. Long interview to promote the film *L'Homme qui ment.* Clear picture of Robbe-Grillet's sense of humor and intelligence.

Fraizer, Dale Watson. *Alain Robbe-Grillet: An Annotated Bibliography of Critical Studies, 1953–1972.* Metuchen, N.J.: The Scarecrow Press, Inc., 1973. Helpful notes on general studies of Robbe-Grillet and on studies of specific novels through *Projet pour une révolution à New York.*

Gardies, André. *Alain Robbe-Grillet.* Cinema d'aujourd'hui 70. Paris: Editions Seghers, 1972. First book-length study of Robbe-Grillet's cinema. Includes stills, interviews, and excerpts from the films.

Genette, Gérard. "Vertige fixé." In *Figures, essais.* Paris: Editions du Seuil, 1966, pp. 69–90. Interesting discussion of the peculiar quality of motionless flux in Robbe-Grillet's novels. Also in *Dans le labyrinthe.* Paris: 10/18, 1959, pp. 273–310.

Goldmann, Lucien. "Nouveau roman et réalité." *Pour une sociologie du roman.* Paris: Gallimard, 1964, pp. 278–333. Important analysis of the New Novel from a Marxist perspective.

Heath, Stephen. *The Nouveau Roman: A Study in the Practice of Writing.* London: Elek, 1972. Excellent chapter on Robbe-Grillet. After situating Robbe-Grillet in an historical, theoretical context of existentialism, phenomenology, and Marxism, Heath discusses the radical intent of Robbe-Grillet's works to challenge traditional reading processes.

Jaffe-Freem, Elly. *Alain Robbe-Grillet et la peinture cubiste.* Amsterdam: Meulenhoff, 1966. Interesting analysis of the similarity of the aims and techniques of Cubist art and of the work of Robbe-Grillet.

Janvier, Ludovic. *Une Parole exigeante.* Paris: Les Editions de Minuit, 1964, pp. 111–46. Chapter on Robbe-Grillet analyzing the opposition of fascination and freedom in terms of the wanderings of Robbe-Grillet's characters in search of a meaning which can or does imprison them.

Jost, François, ed. *Obliques,* no. 16–17 (Fall 1978). Fascinating collection of articles on Robbe-Grillet, interviews with Robbe-Grillet, previously unpublished Robbe-Grillet texts, documents, diagrams for novels and films, photos, collages by Robbe-Grillet, bibliography, and filmography.

Leenhardt, Jacques. *Lecture politique du roman: La Jalousie d'Alain Robbe-Grillet.* Paris: Les Editions de Minuit, 1973. Brilliant study of *La Jalousie* from a Marxist perspective.

Marchand, Jean José. *Archives du 20ème siècle—Alain Robbe-Grillet.* Videocassette available at the Centre Pompidou, Paris, 1971. Seven-hour-long interview done for the French television services in which Robbe-Grillet discusses his personal and professional history.

Matthews, Franklin J. Preface. *La Maison de rendez-vous.* Paris: 10/18, 1972. Interesting discussion of the bases of Robbe-Grillet's creativity.

Morrissette, Bruce. *Intertexual Assemblages in Robbe-Grillet from Topology to the Golden Triangle.* Fredericton, N.B.: York Press, 1979. Extremely helpful and detailed documentation of the sources for Robbe-Grillet's "assembled" novels and descriptive analysis of these novels and the history of their creation.

————. *The Novels of Robbe-Grillet.* Ithaca, N.Y.: Cornell University Press, 1975. Updated version of Morrissette's essential study of

Robbe-Grillet's novels and films through *Projet pour une révolution à New York* and *Glissements progressifs du plaisir.*

Olsen, Karen Yelena. "Anglo-American Critical Reception of Alain Robbe-Grillet." Diss. University of Cincinnati 1976. Very useful bibliography and descriptive analysis.

Rambures, Jean Louis de. Interview. "Comment travaillent les écrivains? Alain Robbe-Grillet: 'Chez moi, c'est la structure qui produit le sens.' " *Le Monde,* 16 January 1975. Interesting description of Robbe-Grillet's method of working.

Ricardou, Jean, and van Rossum-Guyon, Françoise, eds. *Nouveau Roman: hier, aujourd'hui.* 2 vols. Paris: 10/18, 1972. Includes papers presented by both New Novelists and critics plus subsequent debates at the Cerisy colloquium.

Ricardou, Jean. *Pour une théorie du nouveau roman.* Paris: Les Editions de Minuit, 1972. Important article, by the critic whom Robbe-Grillet has called "my loveliest fantasy," on *Projet pour une révolution à New York* describing the use of linguistic and phonetic textual generators.

————, ed. *Robbe-Grillet: Analyse, Théorie.* Colloque de Cerisy. 2 vols. Paris: 10/18, 1976. Collection of papers presented and ensuing debates at Cerisy. Robbe-Grillet's wit and intelligence permeate the discussions recorded in this fascinating document. Several extremely important articles on Robbe-Grillet's work.

Rybalka, Michel. Interview. "Robbe-Grillet artiste joueur." *Le Monde,* 22 September 1978. Helpful discussion of *Souvenirs du triangle d'or* and *Un Régicide.*

Stoltzfus, Ben F. *Alain Robbe-Grillet and the New French Novel.* Carbondale: Southern Illinois University Press, 1964. A traditional, humanist reading of Robbe-Grillet's early works.

Van Wert, William. *The Film Career of Alain Robbe-Grillet.* Boston: G. K. Hall, 1977. Essentially an annotated bibliography, this very useful volume also includes a critical survey and summaries of the films.

————. *The Theory and Practice of the Ciné-Roman.* New York: Arno Press, 1978. Extremely interesting discussion of French avant-garde films. Chapter on techniques used in *Dans le labyrinthe* similar to those used in films.

Index